Fifth Edition

Fluency

Questions, Answers, and Evidence-Based Strategies

Melanie Walski
Peet Smith
Jerry L. Johns
Roberta L. Berglund

Kendall Hunt
publishing company

Book Team

Chairman and Chief Executive Officer   Mark C. Falb
President and Chief Operating Officer   Chad M. Chandlee
Vice President, Higher Education   David L. Tart
Director of Publishing Partnerships   Paul B. Carty
Vice President, Operations   Timothy J. Beitzel
Senior Development Editor   Angela Willenbring
Permissions Editor   Tammy Hunt
Cover Designer   Jenifer Fensterman

Author Information for Correspondence, Professional Development, and Workshops

Melanie Walski, Ph.D.
Assistant Professor
Curriculum and Instruction
Email: *mwalski@niu.edu*

Peet Smith, Ph.D.
Assistant Professor
Curriculum and Instruction
Email: *psmith5@niu.edu*

Jerry L. Johns, Ph.D.
Consultant in Reading
Email: *jjohns@niu.edu*

Roberta L. Berglund, Ed.D.
Consultant in Reading/
Language Arts
Email: *readboulder@yahoo.com*

Ordering Information

Address: Kendall Hunt Publishing Company
                4050 Westmark Drive
                Dubuque, IA 52002
Telephone: 800-247-3458, ext. 4
Web site: www.kendallhunt.com
Fax: 800-772-9165

(Previously titled *Fluency: Differentiated Interventions and Progress-Monitoring Assessments*)

ISBN 978-1-7924-0615-7

Published in the United States of America

Contents

Integrated Strategies
Developing Fluent Readers Incorporating Writing, Speaking, and Listening   115

Appendix A
Answers to Anticipation Guide for Fluency   129

Appendix B
Resources for Assessing and Monitoring Fluency Progress   131

ENTER HERE:
A Quick Orientation to *Fluency*

- **Are you trying to help your students become more fluent readers?**
- **Are you doing progress monitoring?**
- **Do you think that differentiating fluency interventions can help you respond to individual differences among your students?**

Help is on the way. We have written this easy to use resource with you in mind. Our goal is to help you include fluency strategies in your instructional repertoire without adding hours of preparation time.

We wrote *Fluency* for classroom teachers, prospective teachers, reading/literacy specialists and coaches, and other professionals involved in schools and educational agencies. This compact, focused book helps you understand fluency, offers many strategies to strengthen fluency instruction for students in regular classrooms as well as in resource rooms, and provides some ways to help monitor students' progress. Response to Intervention (RTI), part of the 2004 reauthorization of the Individuals with Disabilities Education Act (IDEA), is intended to ensure that all students receive excellent classroom instruction. For those students who struggle, targeted interventions and progress monitoring are used to help assess growth (RTI, 2009).

Part 1: Questions and Answers about Fluency

Part 1 presents a series of questions and answers about fluency. Here you will find helpful and concise answers to common questions teachers have asked about fluency and related areas (e.g., Response to Intervention). We suggest you begin with the Anticipation Guide (page 2) to help activate your background knowledge and ideas about fluency. Next, preview the questions and explore those that relate to your needs and interests. (Note: Answers to statements posed in the Anticipation Guide are provided in Appendix A).

Part 2: Foundational Principles of Fluency Instruction; Evidence-Based Strategies, Activities, and Resources

Part 2 contains a wide range of evidence-based strategies, practical activities, and resources to develop students' fluency at various grade levels. The strategies selected were based on a review of the literature as well as helpful ideas shared by teachers. The strategies are arranged in six areas of classroom practice. See Figure 1.

CLASSROOM PRACTICES FOR FLUENCY

- Building Blocks
- Shared Reading
- Assisted Reading
- Performance Reading
- Independent Reading
- Integrated Strategies

FIGURE 1

Building blocks for fluency contains five important and general foundations for fluency including tips and suggestions for each area. The remaining five areas—**shared reading, assisted reading, performance reading, independent reading**, and **integrated strategies** all have strategies arranged in a similar format:

- Strategy name
- Fluency components
- Materials needed
- Use (whole group, small group, partner, or individual)
- Description
- Step-by-step procedure for teaching the strategy
- Evaluation (student behaviors to look for)
- Considerations (when applicable)

Fluency Walkabout

Materials
- Fluency resources hung up and stored around the classroom (e.g., pocket charts with fluency phrases or sentences, basic sight vocabulary cards; anchor charts with previous fluency lessons; Readers Theater scripts (see page 97); poetry strips; song lyrics from Klassroom Karaoke (see page 86).

Use
- Individual

FLUENCY COMPONENTS
Prosody
Comprehension
Rate
Accuracy

Description

Fluency Walkabouts get students up out of their seats and moving around the classroom. Movement in the classroom has been shown to improve on-task behavior (Mahar, Murphy, Rowe, Golden, Shields, & Raedeke, 2006) and increase students' perceived competence and effort in academic tasks (Vazou, Gavrilou, Mamalaki, Papanastasiou, & Sioumala, 2012). It also reinforces the concept that students need fluency to successfully navigate the spaces around them (e.g., classrooms, schools, communities), and not just a skill needed to read and comprehend books. This activity would be best suited for use during literacy centers in which students are familiar with established routines, including walking around the classroom independently to read various print materials.

Procedure

1. Hang up various fluency materials in easily accessible locations around the classroom. These materials should include texts that students are familiar with, so be sure to save fluency phrases, sentences, basic sight vocabulary cards, and poetry strips to place in pocket charts. You may also want to display anchor charts from previous fluency lessons, scripts from previous Readers Theater lessons and song lyrics from Klassroom Karaoke activities.
2. Model how to (a) navigate the classroom space to access the fluency materials placed around the room, (b) select fluency materials, and (c) practice reading these materials independently and quietly.
3. Allow students to walk freely around the classroom to locate the fluency materials and practice reading them independently. Provide support to students as they first practice these routines.
4. During literacy centers, encourage students to practice the routines of the Fluency Walkabout while they also practice their fluency skills independently.

Evaluation
- Increased confidence reading selected materials
- Navigation of classroom space and activity routines

Considerations
- Be sure to keep materials at students' eye-level so they can access them easily and independently.
- A similar anchor chart or direction sheet as the one used in the Fluency Jars activity (see page 111) with directions on what to do with each type of fluency material may be useful here. An example of one type of activity you could use for a Fluency Walkabout is included on the next page.

The strategies presented later in Part 2 contain a fluency model on the top right corner of the page that indicates which component(s) of fluency (i.e., Prosody, Rate, Accuracy) each strategy targets. Use this model as a guide when deciding which strategy to use with students. For example, if a student struggles with accuracy, look for the model on the top right of each page that emphasizes Accuracy, while Prosody and Rate may be dimmed. This indicates that the strategy mainly focuses on accuracy. Please note that some strategies can target more than one, and sometimes all, of the fluency components. Fluency Walkabout (left) focuses on all three fluency components, so none of the components are dimmed. Note that Comprehension will never be dimmed.

Take a look at the Fluency Walkabout example (left) to see the basic format. Reproducibles are included for many of the strategies.

We receive many positive comments from teachers regarding the organization of the various strategies. We invite your comments as well. Our contact information is given on the copyright page of this book. We also offer professional development services and workshops.

Appendices

Appendix A provides answers to the Anticipation Guide (see page 130). Appendix B offers fluency rubrics and class records to record and monitor students' progress over time.

To summarize, we trust we have provided you with a solid base for understanding fluency by offering numerous ways to help students become confident readers who demonstrate greater fluency and by providing resources to document students' progress in fluency.

About the Authors

Melanie Walski earned her Ph.D. from University of Illinois at Chicago in Curriculum and Instruction with a focus on Language, Literacy, and Culture. Dr. Walski's research includes the impact of policy on literacy instructional practice; the aspects of policy that are most influential on teachers' sensemaking of literacy teaching and learning; and emergent literacy curriculum development. Dr. Walski was a teacher in the Los Angeles Unified School District in California, a reading specialist at Dominican University in Illinois, and a literacy consultant in Chicago. Dr. Walski currently is an assistant professor at Northern Illinois University where she teaches literacy courses at both the undergraduate and graduate levels.

Photo by Peet Smith

Peet Smith earned her Ph.D. from University of Maryland, College Park in Special Education with a focus on Literacy and Reading. Dr. Smith's research interests include upper elementary and middle school students' engagement in literacy learning, particularly English Learners' and struggling readers' engagement in reading expository texts. She has taught elementary and middle school reading at a parochial school in Philadelphia, PA and a charter school Lubbock, TX. Dr. Smith is currently an assistant professor in the Department of Curriculum and Instruction at Northern Illinois University.

Photo by Kevin Zieber

Jerry L. Johns has been recognized as a distinguished teacher, writer, outstanding teacher educator, and popular professional development speaker for schools, school districts, and conferences. He has taught students from kindergarten through graduate school and also served as a reading teacher. Professor Johns spent his career at Northern Illinois University. He served in leadership positions at the local, state, national, and international levels. He has been president of the International Literacy Association, the Illinois Reading Council, the Association of Literacy Educators and Researchers, and the Northern Illinois Reading Council. He also served on the Board of Directors for each of these organizations as well as the American Reading Forum. Dr. Johns has authored or coauthored nearly 300 articles, monographs, and research studies as well as over 40 professional books. His *Basic Reading Inventory*, now in the 12th edition, is widely used in undergraduate and graduate classes as well as by practicing teachers.

© Kristine H. Wilke

Used with permission. © Lifetouch Inc.

Roberta L. (Bobbi) Berglund has received honors for outstanding service throughout her career, which includes serving as a classroom teacher, reading specialist, ELL resource teacher, director of Title I programs, and director of literacy. Dr. Berglund has also been a member of the reading faculty at the University of Wisconsin-Whitewater and has taught undergraduate and graduate reading courses at Northern Illinois University, Rockford University, National Louis University, and Aurora University. Dr. Berglund has worked with school districts and state education agencies in developing curriculum materials, assessments, and leading professional development programs. She has been a speaker at state, national, and international conferences and a leader in professional organizations. Dr. Berglund is the author of over 50 publications and is the author or coauthor of 15 professional books.

PART 1

Questions and Answers about Fluency

Overview and Anticipation Guide

This part of the book provides a series of questions and answers related to fluency. We have also provided an anticipation guide so you can react to some statements about fluency before reading the book.

Anticipation Guide for Fluency

Read the statements below and check those with which you agree. Note: Answers are provided in Appendix A.

BEFORE READING

Agree	Disagree	
_____	_____	1. The role of fluency in reading programs has remained the same over the years.
_____	_____	2. Fluency is independent of comprehension.
_____	_____	3. Fluency in reading is most relevant at the beginning stages of reading.
_____	_____	4. It is appropriate to consider fluency in silent reading.
_____	_____	5. One aspect of fluency can be judged by determining the student's rate of reading in words per minute (WPM).
_____	_____	6. A reasonable oral fluency rate for third-grade students is 160 words correct per minute (WCPM) by the end of the school year.
_____	_____	7. Rate of reading is the most important component of fluency.
_____	_____	8. Fluency should be assessed informally as part of the regular classroom routine.
_____	_____	9. Round-robin oral reading is an effective fluency activity.
_____	_____	10. Fluency strategies are primarily for students experiencing difficulty in reading.
_____	_____	11. Research has identified several methods to increase reading fluency.
_____	_____	12. Oral reading fluency is developed best through independent reading.
_____	_____	13. Fluency instruction should begin after students have established conventional reading, typically in second grade.
_____	_____	14. Some teacher behaviors can contribute to students' dysfluency in reading.
_____	_____	15. Fluency strategies and interventions can be differentiated.

1. Why Another Book on Fluency?

You may be asking yourself why another book on fluency and why now. We asked ourselves the same question as we set out to revise this book. It may seem in the age of Common Core State Standards (National Governors Association Center for Best Practices, 2010) and the demands it puts on teachers and students to shift away from focusing on developing skills to developing deep and critical comprehension abilities, that fluency is a relic of a simpler time. For many years it had been ranked as *Not Hot* on the annual *What's Hot in Literacy Report* (International Literacy Association, 2018). Now it is no longer it's own topic, but lumped into Early Literacy along with phonemic awareness, phonics, vocabulary, and comprehension. And, like many things we take for granted, fluency may no longer be a hot topic, but it remains a critical component to building the foundation of reading. In fact, while the Common Core may focus on developing critical consumers and producers of literacy, it also acknowledges the importance of fluency by dedicating an entire strand to the skill. However, an important point of the fluency standards (i.e., CCSS.ELA-LITERACY.RF.4) is the emphasis on developing fluency to support comprehension. Fluency, as outlined in the K–5 Reading Foundational standards, does not dictate a specific word per minute score. What it does outline is the importance of reading with sufficient accuracy, rate, and expression to help students build their capacity for comprehension. In other words, fluency is the result of students building their other foundational reading skills (i.e., print concepts, phonological awareness, phonics, and word recognition). Fluency should be seen as the result of skill development and the conduit to comprehension. Without fluent reading, students will have a much harder time understanding complex text.

2. What Is Fluency?

Fluency has been defined in multiple ways according to different theoretical perspectives (Kuhn, Schwanenflugel, Meisinger, Levy, & Rasinski, 2010). We define fluency as the ability to read without having to devote excessive cognitive energy to decoding so the reader is able to focus on making meaning of the text. The National Reading Panel report (2000), brought fluency into the spotlight for early reading development as an essential element of reading instruction. In fact, once fluency became one of the "Five Pillars" (National Reading Panel, 2000) of reading instruction, schools across the country devoted more instructional time and assessment resources to the skill. However, as time has passed, teachers have come to understand that fluency as measured by accuracy, rate, and prosody are nothing without the end result being comprehension.

Although fluency pertains to both oral and silent reading, fluency is often associated with oral reading, because teachers can observe accuracy by recording the number of miscues the student makes while reading and can also note the student's rate, phrasing, and expression. Generally, it is assumed that oral reading is similar, but not identical, to students' silent reading. Speed and comprehension can be evaluated in both oral and silent reading. You might find it useful to think of fluency as having three components: 1) accuracy, 2) rate, and 3) prosody with the end goal being comprehension. See Figure 1.1.

While comprehension is the end goal, the other dimensions of fluency are essential to reaching that goal. **Accuracy** describes the student's ability to correctly decode a word. Ideally, students develop automaticity of most or all of the

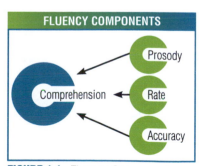

FIGURE 1.1. Fluency Components

Fluency is related to reading comprehension.

words they will encounter in a text (Samuels, 2002, 2006). To be an accurate reader, students need to have both a large sight vocabulary as well as a range of decoding skills. As students move from emergent to beginning reader (White-hurst & Lonigan, 1998) their accuracy will improve as they have internalized decoding rules and have had more experience with reading conventionally. It should be expected that students will make some miscues (for example, mispronouncing, omitting, or inserting words) during reading. This is a typical occurrence in reading development. According to many guided reading level programs, if the student misses more than 10% of the words in a passage (one word in ten), the text material is probably too difficult to use for instruction (Johns, Elish-Piper, & Johns, 2017).

Rate refers to the speed of reading, usually determined in words per minute (WPM) or words correct per minute (WCPM). "A consensus exists among researchers that reading rate is a crucial factor in determining reading fluency at all levels" (Breznitz, 2006, p. 9). This is because rate is directly connected to the student's ability to decode the words in the text. A slower rate indicates a student has to exert cognitive energy on decoding the word, and a faster rate indicates that automaticity is developing. "WCPM has been shown . . . to serve as an accurate and powerful indicator of overall reading competence, especially in its strong correlation with comprehension" (Hasbrouck & Tindal, 2006, p. 636).

Reading rate is a crucial factor in determining reading fluency at all levels.

Prosody refers to the rhythm, stress, phrasing, and intonation of speech (Cowie, Douglas-Cowie, & Wichmann, 2002; Miller & Schwanenflugel, 2006, 2008; Schwanenflugel, Hamilton, Kuhn, Wisenbaker & Stahl, 2004). As students strengthen accuracy and automatic word reading, their cognitive energy shifts to comprehension which allows them to read aloud in a way that sounds like natural speech. When oral reading occurs with those natural sounding speech patterns, we assume that students comprehend the words in order to produce them in a prosodic way. Note the slashes in the following sentence; they provide an example of what proper expression would approximate when read aloud.

The frisky dog/ ran quickly/ to the front door.

Comprehension refers to understanding. Without comprehension, reading is merely word calling or barking at print. Comprehension is usually evaluated through retelling, answering questions, discussion, drawing/art, dramatic interpretation, or some combination of these methods. Fluency is related to reading comprehension, so the ability of students to read quickly, accurately, and smoothly helps improve comprehension. In some schools and classrooms, however, so much emphasis is placed on speed and accuracy that comprehension suffers. Applegate, Applegate, and Modla (2009) found that one third of the strong fluent readers in their study "struggled mightily with comprehension" leading to the conclusion that many of the students "had been judged strong readers on the basis of their pacing [speed], accuracy, and prosody [expression] alone" (p. 518).

3. Why Is Fluency Important?

In essence, students who are fluent readers are better able to devote their attention to comprehending the text. LaBerge and Samuels (1974) presented the basic theory underlying fluency. A student has only so much attention to focus on comprehension. As more and more of that attention is devoted to recognizing words, the result is likely to be limited reading fluency and comprehension. Fluency, then, generally results in increased comprehension.

There are other reasons why fluency is important. Students in elementary, middle, and high school who experience difficulty in reading, for the most part, lack fluency. To help students who struggle in reading, attention in the instructional program should be devoted to fluency. "It is generally acknowledged that fluency is a critical component of skilled reading" (National Reading Panel, 2000, p. 3-1). For example, Shanahan (2000), in his framework for literacy instruction, identifies fluency as one of the major components. Heilman, Blair, and Rupley (2002) also identify fluency as a major instructional task. Fluency with text also helps to affirm and support the student's positive perception as a reader. Students who are fluent "can process more words and more text," and more reading promotes greater reading growth (McCormick, 2007, p. 256).

Fluency is a critical component of skilled reading.

4. How Does Oral Reading Fluency Relate to Silent Reading Fluency?

Fluency is often thought about in relation to oral reading; nevertheless, fluency is also important in silent reading if students are to be efficient and effective readers. Silent reading also becomes more important as students progress through the grades. Ultimately, most of the reading done by students and adults is silent reading. Because silent reading is used so commonly, the rate at which students comprehend is an important instructional consideration (Hiebert, Samuels, & Rasinski, 2012).

Carver (1989) has provided some helpful information on silent reading rates. The figures he provides are the average reading rates of students in a particular grade who can understand material at that grade level. Note that rate is considered in tandem with comprehension or understanding. Carver presents his rate figures in standard word lengths, but you can determine a student's rate (which we answer in the next question) and compare it to the figures in Table 1. Such a comparison will give you an indication of how the student's rate compares with the rates at which average students in a particular grade read with understanding.

5. How Is Rate of Reading Determined?

Reading rate is often reported in words per minute (WPM) or words correct per minute (WCPM). The same basic procedure can be used for oral and silent reading. Basically, the procedure involves having the student read a selection while you time the reading, using a stopwatch or a watch with a second hand. The following steps will permit you to determine a student's rate of reading in WPM. See the example in Figure 1.2 on the next page.

1. Count or estimate the number of words in the selection. If the passage is short (175 words or less), actually count the words. If the passage is longer, you can estimate the number of words by counting the number of words on a representative line of text and counting the number of lines. Then you multiply the two numbers to get an estimate of the number of words in the passage. For example, if there are 30 lines in the passage,

TABLE 1

Silent Reading Rates for Students Who Understand the Material	
GRADE	WPM
1	<81
2	82–108
3	109–130
4	131–147
5	148–161
6	162–174
7	175–185
8	186–197
9	198–209
10	210–224
11	225–240
12	241–255

FIGURE 1.2

with 10 words on a representative line, there would be approximately 300 words ($30 \times 10 = 300$) in the passage.

2. Multiply by 60 ($300 \times 60 = 18000$). This step is necessary to determine WPM.

3. This numeral becomes the dividend (18000).

4. Time the student's reading in seconds (e.g., 90 seconds).

5. This numeral becomes the divisor (90).

6. Do the necessary division. The resulting numeral is the quotient, which is words per minute (WPM).

If the resulting numeral is based on silent reading, use Table 1. If the student reads orally, use Table 2 presented in the next section.

You will notice that Table 2 uses words **correct** per minute (WCPM) in reporting oral reading rates. To determine WCPM, follow the same six steps outlined above. Once you determine WPM, total and subtract the number of mispronunciations, substitutions, omissions, reversals, and pauses on words for at least three seconds (pronounce the word for the student after three seconds). The result will be WCPM. For example, if a student achieves a rate of 137 WPM but makes two mispronunciations, one substitution, and two omissions, there are five miscues. You merely subtract these five miscues from 137. The result is 132 WCPM.

6. What Oral Reading Rates Are Provided by Research?

The answer to this straightforward question is more complex than it appears. One reason for this complexity is that there is no consensus in the literature (Bear & Barone, 1998; Kuhn & Stahl, 2000; Rasinski & Padak, 1996). Another reason is that classrooms and schools can differ in many variables that impact so-called average oral reading rates. Perhaps the best advice is to develop local norms for different grade levels. Such advice, however, means more work for school personnel. The results of such efforts, if undertaken in a thoughtful and consistent manner, will provide meaningful and useful data. However, while setting local norms can be helpful in documenting the achievement of students in the local population, concerns can arise when the academic skills of the local student population is lower than what is considered typical, average, or desired.

To help teachers who may not have the time or desire to establish local norms for oral reading rates, Table 2 provides norms for grades one through six based on the research of Hasbrouck and Tindal (2017). These researchers compiled scores from three commercially produced and widely used oral reading fluency assessments (i.e., DIBELS 6th edition©, DIBELS Next©, and easyCBM©) to establish updated oral reading norms for students in grades one through six. The norms provide words correct per minute (WCPM) at the 10th, 25th, 50th, 75th, and 90th percentiles for students in grades two through six at three points (fall, winter, and spring) during the school year. The numbers of scores used to compile these norms are provided in Table 3. Please note that scores collected from DIBELS 6th edition and DIBELS Next include those from all students completing the Oral Reading Fluency (ORF) assessment while easyCBM developers used a stratified random sampling (Hasbrouck & Tindal, 2017). Due to the

TABLE 2

Oral Reading Norms for Students in Grades One through Six
(Hasbrouck & Tindal, 2017)

GRADE	PERCENTILE	WCPM		
		FALL	WINTER	SPRING
1	90		97	116
	75		59	91
	50	NA	29	60
	25		16	34
	10		9	18
2	90	111	131	148
	75	84	109	124
	50	50	84	100
	25	36	59	72
	10	23	35	43
3	90	134	161	166
	75	104	137	139
	50	83	97	112
	25	59	79	91
	10	40	62	63
4	90	153	169	184
	75	125	143	160
	50	94	120	133
	25	75	95	105
	10	60	71	83
5	90	179	183	195
	75	153	160	169
	50	121	133	146
	25	87	109	119
	10	64	84	102
6	90	185	195	204
	75	159	166	173
	50	132	145	146
	25	112	116	122
	10	89	91	91
7*	90	180	192	202
	75	156	165	177
	50	128	136	150
	25	102	109	123
	10	79	88	98
8*	90	185	199	199
	75	161	173	177
	50	133	146	151
	25	106	115	124
	10	77	84	97

*Oral Reading Norms for Students in Grades Seven and Eight (Hasbrouck & Tindal, 2006)

TABLE 3

Number of Student Scores Used In the Hasbrouck and Tindal Fluency Norms for Grades One through Six

GRADE	FALL			WINTER			SPRING		
	D6	DN	EZ	D6	DN	EZ	D6	DN	EZ
1	NA	NA	NA	660,404	4,612	500	651,275	4,495	500
2	637,017	4,231	500	615,480	4,311	500	608,782	4,176	500
3	523,144	3,855	500	502,368	3,889	500	496,638	3,777	500
4	346,306	3,772	500	325,664	3,840	500	323,097	3,648	500
5	288,493	2,409	500	264,345	2,435	500	264,536	2,393	500
6	113,298	1,456	500	100,537	1,485	500	100,430	1,484	500
Totals	1,908,258	15,723	2,500	2,468,798	20,572	3000	2,444,758	19,973	3,000
Overall Totals	1,926,481			2,492,370			2,467,731		

Note: D6 = DIBELS 6th edition©, DN = DIBELS Next©, and EZ = easyCBM©

From *Behavioral Research & Teaching, Technical Report #1702: An Update to Compiled ORF Norms* by Jan Hasbrouck and Gerald Tindal. Copyright © 2017 by University of Oregon. Reprinted by permission.

available data, Hasbrouck and Tindal did not calculate norms for grades seven and eight as they had previously (Hasbrouck & Tindal, 2006). We have included the norms established in 2006 for grades seven and eight.

7. How Should the Norms for Oral Reading Be Used?

The information in Table 2 can provide one basis for judging students' rates, but there are two important points to keep in mind when using the oral reading norms provided in this book or from other sources.

First, and most important, oral reading rates should not be considered synonymous with fluency. Rate is *one* of the three components of fluency; the other two are accuracy and prosody. Failure to take each of these components into account can lead to distortions of a more complete construct of fluency (Rasinski, 2006). For example, a student who has a high reading rate with minimal comprehension will need a different sort of instruction than a student with a slow reading rate who has excellent comprehension. Even a student who reads orally very quickly with good comprehension may need some instruction on expressive oral reading, perhaps using strategies like Reading Punctuation (page 55), Guess the Emotion (page 90), and Phrased Reading (page 57). You should tailor students' instruction according to their individual needs by first pinpointing which components of fluency a student has the strongest understanding and which areas a student may need additional support. Identifying these areas of strength and need will help you to create different types of instruction to boost students' overall fluency.

Second, there are several important variables that can impact fluency—such as the type of text. Texts can be broadly characterized as narrative and informational. It is likely that a student will have more fluent reading with a story or with

Norms provide helpful information to teachers who desire some guidelines for students' reading rates.

Oral reading rates should not be considered synonymous with fluency.

a selection from informational text about which they already possess a great deal of background knowledge. The student's purpose for reading may also impact fluency. The common one-minute reads used by many schools to determine rate may predispose some students to get through the passage quickly without a concern for accuracy, prosody, and/or comprehension. In addition, the sustainability of a particular rate during "normal" reading is probably suspect. Unfortunately, fluency norms give no attention to these important variables, so it is up to you to be mindful of them when assessing oral reading rate and using fluency norms.

8. What Are Some Ways to Assess Fluency?

Accuracy and speed can often be confused with being the only components of fluency development, often ignoring the dimension of prosody that includes author expressiveness and phrasing (Daane, Campbell, Grigg, Goodman, & Oranje, 2005). To help remedy this situation, we suggest a combination of quantitative (numbers) and qualitative (behaviors) criteria. There are often numbers related to reading rate expressed in words per minute (WPM) or words correct per minute (WCPM). Tables 1 and 2 contain numbers that can be used in a quantitative manner. You can also keep track of how accurately a student reads by counting the number of miscues (e.g., mispronunciations, repetitions, insertions, substitutions, and omissions) made during the reading of a passage. You should also assess the student's comprehension by asking comprehension questions, using retelling, or a combination of questions and retelling. Recommendations for the evaluation of students' fluency progress are included in each activity in Part 2 of this book. For example, the method of Structured Repeated Reading (page 70) offers one way to help judge a student's progress as the same passage is reread over a period of days.

Examples of qualitative behaviors that can be assessed are:

- voice quality
- expression and emphasis
- phrasing and pauses
- appropriate attention to and use of punctuation

Some teachers develop informal fluency rubrics that can be used to judge aspects of fluency. We have provided three such rubrics in Appendix B that you may wish to use. The first is a Four-Point Fluency Rubric that contains both quantitative and qualitative criteria. The second fluency rubric (Four-Point Fluency Rubric for Oral Reading) focuses specifically on oral reading behaviors (i.e., rate, expression, phrasing, punctuation). The third fluency rubric (Holistic Oral Reading Fluency Scale) also focuses on oral reading.

The Classroom Fluency Snapshot (CFS), developed by Blachowicz, Sullivan, and Cieply (2001) and expanded by Moskal and Blachowicz (2006), offers another way to assess fluency. This assessment shows clearly how a student's reading rate compares with others in the classroom. The CFS can be used in the fall of the school year to help establish baseline data for the class. Subsequent snapshots can be used throughout the year to measure and monitor student progress. The chart in Figure 1.3 shows an example from a second-grade classroom. Charts for your use can be found in Appendix B. On the next page is an adapted step-by-step procedure for using the CFS with a class of students.

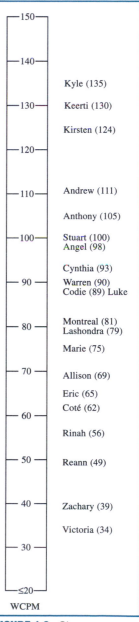

FIGURE 1.3. Classroom Fluency Snapshot

1. Select a passage that is representative of the material you will use for instruction. All students will read the same passage, so make sufficient teacher copies for your use. The majority of students should be able to read the passage with at least 85% to 90% initial accuracy. Choose a passage that will take students one or two minutes to read. Although the passage will be difficult for some of your developing readers, you will be able to establish baseline data for the entire class.

Materials Needed

- Provide a copy of the passage for the student to read.
- Have a copy of the passage on which you will mark miscues (any deviation from what's written) such as omissions, insertions, mispronunciations, ignoring or adding punctuation, and words pronounced after waiting three seconds. You may mark the actual miscues where they occur in the text if you are familiar with coding miscues or use a running record procedure. A method for coding miscues can be found below.

Miscues that Count as Errors

Mispronunciation	*scrape* scrap
Substitution	*pet* pat
Omission	~~pen~~
Reversal	*no* on
Insertion	*cute* ^cat
Pause (3 seconds)	*P* reality (after 3 seconds word is read)

Miscues that Do Not Count as Errors

Repetition	<u>little</u>
Self-correction	*mark SC* mask
Dialect	*pin* pen

- Use a timer to time the student's reading.
- Use a voice recorder if you wish to do the analysis later or recheck your coding of miscues and the number of seconds taken for reading.

2. Invite individual students to read the passage to you. You could offer an introductory statement like: "Please read this passage about _____ at a speed that's just right for you. Read as accurately as you can. When you have finished reading, I'll ask you a few questions (or I'll ask you to retell what you have read)." At the end of one minute, make a mark after the last word read by the student. Invite a short retelling or ask some questions based on the selection.

3. Count the number of words read in one minute and then subtract the number of miscues (e.g., mispronunciations, substitutions, omissions, reversals, and ignored punctuation). An easy way to determine word counts is to place a numeral at the end of each line to indicate the cumulative number of words. Use this information to quickly determine the number of words the student read and then subtract the number of miscues to determine words correct per minute. A partial sample is shown in Figure 1.4.

At the Farm

wanted

Sue was visiting her grandparents' farm for a week. She decided to have a picnic   *15*

in the woods. She packed a lunch with a peanut-butter and jelly sandwich, an apple,   *31*

The

When she remembered|Jane. She ran back to the house and got Jane, her favorite doll.   *108*

end of one minute

Name _*Stacy*_____   Date _____*9-29-2020*_____

Total Words Read   __*95*__   Additional Notes/Comments: *good phrasing*

Number of Miscues   __*2*__

Words Correct per Minute __*93*__

FIGURE 1.4

---

4. Compile the results for all the students on a sample chart like that shown in Figure 1.3 to see the range of rates in your class and to help determine which students might benefit from instruction to improve fluency. Repeating the process several times during the school year (see Figure 1.5) with the same or different passages should enable you to assess individual and class progress. There are two blank charts provided for your use in Appendix B. One chart is for the primary grades; the other chart is for the upper grades.

9. What's Wrong with Round-Robin Oral Reading?

Round-robin oral reading is "the outmoded practice of calling on students to read orally one after the other" (Harris & Hodges, 1995, p. 222). It often refers to oral reading done at sight in the context of whole class or small group instruction and looks something like this: "Class, turn to page 53 in your books. José, you begin reading. I want the rest of the class to follow along." As José reads, some students are reading ahead, some are actually following along, and others are looking out the window or daydreaming. You may even recall some of your own experiences with round-robin oral reading.

So what's wrong with round-robin oral reading? Ash and Kuhn (2006) note that "it runs counter to research on good literacy instruction" (p. 156). Here's our list of common objections to the practice:

Round-robin oral reading rarely fulfills the purposes of oral reading.

- It focuses mostly on oral reading performance, rather than comprehension.
- It rarely engages students (except the student who is reading).

Reading Rates in WCPM for a Grade Two Classroom

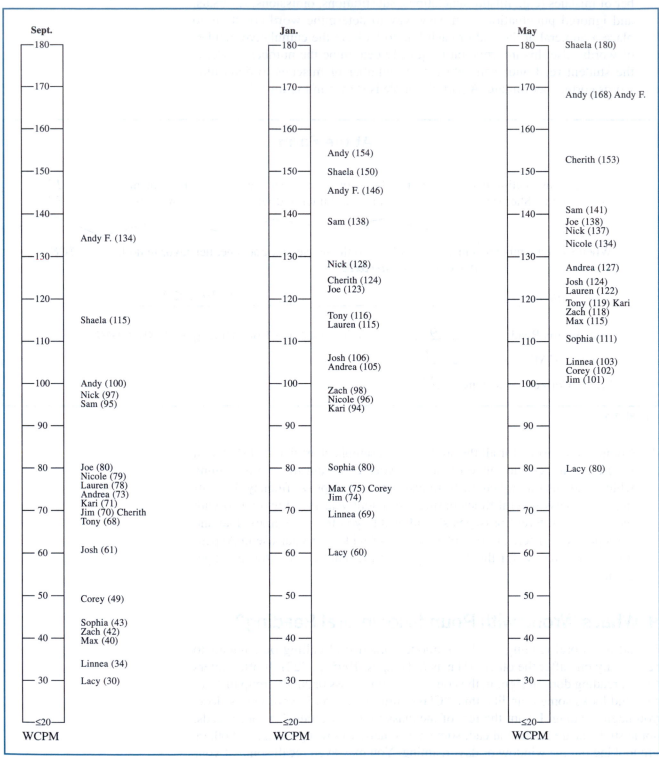

Sept.

- 180
- 170
- 160
- 150
- 140
- Andy F. (134) — 130
- 120
- Shaela (115) — 110
- 100 — Andy (100) / Nick (97) / Sam (95)
- 90
- 80 — Joe (80) / Nicole (79) / Lauren (78) / Andrea (73) / Kari (71) / Jim (70) Cherith / Tony (68)
- 70
- 60 — Josh (61)
- 50 — Corey (49)
- 40 — Sophia (43) / Zach (42) / Max (40)
- Linnea (34)
- 30 — Lacy (30)
- ≤20

WCPM

Jan.

- 180
- 170
- 160
- Andy (154) — 150
- Shaela (150)
- Andy F. (146)
- 140 — Sam (138)
- 130 — Nick (128) / Cherith (124) / Joe (123)
- 120 — Tony (116) / Lauren (115)
- 110 — Josh (106) / Andrea (105)
- 100 — Zach (98) / Nicole (96) / Kari (94)
- 90
- 80 — Sophia (80) / Max (75) Corey / Jim (74)
- 70 — Linnea (69)
- 60 — Lacy (60)
- 50
- 40
- 30
- ≤20

WCPM

May

- 180 — Shaela (180)
- 170 — Andy (168) Andy F.
- 160
- 150 — Cherith (153)
- 140 — Sam (141) / Joe (138) / Nick (137) / Nicole (134)
- 130 — Andrea (127) / Josh (124) / Lauren (122)
- 120 — Tony (119) Kari / Zach (118) / Max (115)
- 110 — Sophia (111) / Linnea (103) / Corey (102) / Jim (101)
- 100
- 90
- 80 — Lacy (80)
- 70
- 60
- 50
- 40
- 30
- ≤20

WCPM

FIGURE 1.5

- It reduces the amount of time all students could be engaged in reading.
- It reduces the time that could be better spent on quality instructional practices.
- It puts pressure on developing readers who may struggle with oral reading.

According to Hyatt (1943), who traced the history and development of oral reading over a sixty-year period, oral reading is worthwhile only when it 1) informs or entertains an audience; 2) enables students to participate in a group activity (such as choral reading); or 3) increases one's personal pleasure by reading aloud beautiful passages of literature. Unfortunately, round-robin oral reading rarely, if ever, fulfills any of these three purposes.

When it comes to fluency, there is no doubt that *meaningful oral reading is important*. A study by Eldredge, Reutzel, and Hollingsworth (1996) found that round-robin oral reading was inferior to the shared book experience in reducing students' miscues, improving reading fluency, increasing vocabulary acquisition, and improving reading comprehension. In Part 2 of this book, we offer a number of oral reading practices that promote fluency without the negatives generally associated with round-robin oral reading. Additional ideas can be found in Opitz and Rasinski (2008).

10. What Part of the Reading Program Should Be Devoted to Fluency Instruction?

"Fluency is one critical aspect of proficient reading" (Allington, 2009, p. 49). In a position statement of the International Literacy Association (2018), the ability to read fluently is among the skills students need to become readers. Shanahan (2000) suggests that up to 25% of the instructional time for reading should be focused on fluency instruction. That percentage may be high, but it is clear that fluency should be an important component of the reading program. Once viewed as neglected, fluency now seems to have gained an over-emphasis in many schools' reading programs. The amount of time devoted to fluency instruction may depend on the grade level and the student's facility with word identification. It is important to consider the use of fluency strategies in each area of a balanced reading program: reading aloud, shared reading, guided reading, and independent reading. Most of the strategies in this book can be used in one or more of these areas. It is important to remember that fluency strategies can also be practiced and used in the content areas not only to improve fluency, but also to increase comprehension and the enjoyment of reading informational text.

In the Common Core Standards for English Language Arts, fluency is a standard found in the Reading Foundational strand. From kindergarten to fifth grade, students are expected to build their fluency abilities while matching the demands of complex text appropriate for their grade. Below are the standards for each grade.

Kindergarten CCSS.ELA.RF.4. Read emergent-reader texts with purpose and understanding.

Grades 1–2 CCSS.ELA.RF.4. Read with sufficient accuracy and fluency to support comprehension. a) Read grade-level text with purpose and understanding. b) Read grade-level text orally with accuracy, appropriate rate, and expression on successive readings. c) Use context to confirm or self-correct word recognition and understanding, rereading as necessary.

The ability to read fluently is among the skills students need to become proficient readers.

Grades 3–5 CCSS.ELA.RF.4. Read with sufficient accuracy and fluency to support comprehension. a) Read grade-level text with purpose and understanding. b) Read grade-level prose and poetry orally with accuracy, appropriate rate, and expression on successive readings. c) Use context to confirm or self-correct word recognition and understanding, rereading as necessary.

Reading the standards for fluency, it is clear that students are expected to develop fluency with grade-level texts with sufficient accuracy, rate, and expression (i.e., prosody) in order to support comprehension. Specific oral reading rates are not outlined in the standards, but instead emphasize the importance of purpose and understanding. As students progress through the grades, fluency expectations increase. That is, increases in fluency expectations are apparent from emergent reading (kindergarten), to oral reading with grade-level texts (Grades 1–2), and finally to prose and poetry texts (Grades 3–5) with sufficient accuracy rate, and expression to support comprehension. The CCSS-ELA does not include fluency standards beyond fifth grade.

While the Common Core State Standards are not mandated, a majority of states and territories of the U.S. have adopted them for English Language Arts (see corestandards.org for more information). States that have not adopted the standards developed their own fluency standards, many of which are based on the language found in the CCSS-ELA standards for fluency (e.g., Florida, Alaska, and Indiana).

State standards continue to include student expectations for fluency because of the link between developing the component skills of fluency with comprehension. A study with students in grades three, five, and seven by Rasinski, Rikli, and Johnston (2009) reported moderately strong correlations (.57–.66) between measures of oral reading fluency and silent reading comprehension. Such findings suggest that fluency appears to be an important variable in students' reading in elementary grades that continues in the upper grades and middle school.

> Fluency also appears to be an important variable in students' reading in the upper grades and middle school.

Fluency in high school has also been investigated. One study (Rasinski, Padak, McKeon, Wilfong, Friedauer, & Heim, 2005) explored the decoding accuracy and reading rates of over 300 ninth graders in an urban high school. Students read a ninth-grade passage for one minute and then retold what they had read. The researchers found that students read with an average 97.4 percent in decoding accuracy and a reading rate of 136.4 words correct per minute. The average reading rate of these students was "below the 25th percentile *for eighth graders*" (p. 24). In addition, the reading fluency levels were correlated (r=.53) to students' comprehension performance. Although correlation does not imply causation, the findings led the researchers to conclude that reading fluency "needs to be considered even among high school students, and especially among struggling readers" (p. 25).

11. What Insights Can Be Drawn from Research and Expert Opinion?

The most recent National Assessment of Educational Progress data for 2017 revealed that approximately 37% of fourth-grade students performed at the *Proficient* or *Advanced* levels on the reading assessment. This suggests that many students do not have adequate fluency to read grade-level material (Pinnell, Pikulski, Wixson, Campbell, Gough, & Beatty, 1995; Rasinski, 2017). There has been increased emphasis on research-based and evidenced-based practices related to reading and particularly fluency development. Kuhn and Stahl (2000) reviewed over forty studies related to fluency and concluded that "both assisted and unassisted methods of fluency instruction have been generally effective in facilitating rate and accuracy" (p. 25). Some of the studies also found improvements in students' comprehension.

After reviewing many studies, the contributors to the Report of the National Reading Panel (2000) noted that fluency can be improved for good readers as well as readers who struggle. "Classroom practices that encourage repeated oral reading with feedback and guidance lead to meaningful improvements in reading expertise for students" (National Reading Panel, 2000, p. 3-3). One way to judge the impact of guided oral reading procedures is to look at the effect size—the extent to which performance of the treatment group is greater than the performance of the control group. Effect sizes can be small (.20), moderate (.50), or large (.80). Table 4 shows the effect sizes for reading accuracy, fluency, and comprehension. "These data provide strong support for the supposition that instruction in guided oral reading is effective in improving reading" (National Reading Panel, 2000, p. 3-3).

Repeated oral reading with feedback and guidance leads to improvement in reading.

TABLE 4

Effect Sizes of Repeated Oral Reading with Feedback on Three Reading Outcomes	
READING OUTCOME	EFFECT SIZE
Reading Accuracy	.55
Reading Fluency	.44
Reading Comprehension	.35

Klenk and Kibby (2000) also reviewed fluency research. They found that repeated reading was a common method of developing fluency, especially for students in the primary grades. They also noted that teacher modeling of the text students were about to read was another practice used to promote fluency. There are also many research studies (see Pearson & Fielding, 1991, for a review) that have shown relationships between the amount of reading students engage in and reading achievement. Allington (2009, p. 82) notes that "the evidence is quite clear that it takes a lot of reading to become a good reader." Such findings suggest that recreational reading and other independent reading (like Sustained Silent Reading) in and out of school are important considerations in any efforts to increase fluency. Some specific procedures were also highlighted in the reviews of research (e.g., Repeated Reading, Neurological Impress, and Paired Reading), so we have included them in Part 2 of the book.

12. What Factors Can Impact Fluency?

The most fundamental and important basis for fluency is accuracy in word recognition. The significance of this area was pointed out by Anderson, Hiebert, Scott, and Wilkinson (1985, p. 36), who noted that "one of the cornerstones of skilled reading is fast, accurate word identification." When the student recognizes most of the words quickly and easily, they are called sight words. While word recognition is necessary, it is not a sufficient indicator of fluent reading.

The most important basis for fluency is accuracy in word recognition.

Other factors can also impact fluency:

- Reading widely and often provides practice to solidify skills and helps promote confidence in reading.

- Opportunities to participate in meaningful activities for oral reading provide helpful models and practice.

- Listening to teachers read aloud on a daily basis provides an excellent model, enlarges students' vocabularies (Elley, 1988; Layne, 1996), and helps promote the value of reading.

• Providing access to easy, interesting books that can be self-selected by students will encourage voluntary reading.

There are also many direct and indirect actions you can take to teach and promote fluency. We present many of these actions, lessons, and tips in Part 2.

13. When Should Fluency Instruction Begin?

According to Kuhn and Stahl's review of research involving practices for developmental and striving readers (2000), students need to have some basic reading ability before instruction focuses on fluency. Generally, this ability involves knowledge of sight vocabulary and an understanding of how print works. Students typically achieve this ability at the late pre-primer level. Older students who read at a late second-grade level or lower can also profit from fluency instruction. In addition, Worthy and Broaddus (2001/2002) note that fluency practice can also be used with older students to contribute to their comprehension and enjoyment of a wide range of textual materials. Although fluency instruction can generally begin in the second half of first grade, it is appropriate for students at any grade level who struggle with fluency.

Students need to have some basic reading ability before instruction focuses on fluency.

14. What Are the Basic Principles of Fluency Instruction?

Our review of the research, extensive reading, workshops with teachers, and professional experience led to the formulation of the following set of foundational principles related to fluency instruction.

1. Fluency is one of three core elements of skilled reading; the other two are identifying words and constructing meaning. For students, fluency is the bridge or link between the ability to identify words quickly and the ability to understand text. If students read fluently, they can focus most of their attention on the meaningful and enjoyable aspects of reading (Burns, Griffin, & Snow, 1999). Figure 1.6 shows the role fluency plays in skilled reading.

Fluency is the bridge between the ability to identify words and the ability to understand text.

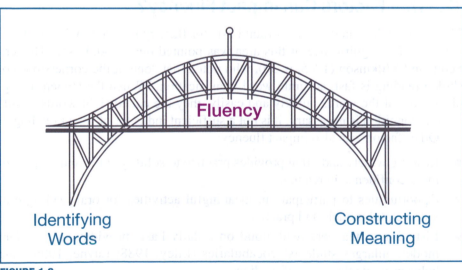

Fluency

Identifying Words

Constructing Meaning

FIGURE 1.6

2. Fluency is linked to comprehension. The impact of oral reading practice, feedback, and guidance on comprehension "is not inconsiderable, and in several comparisons it was actually quite high" (National Reading Panel, 2000, p. 3-18). Although there is reason to believe that oral reading practice and feedback have an impact on comprehension, we want to stress the importance of assessing comprehension or inviting retellings. Students need to understand that the goal of reading is the construction of meaning—not merely pronouncing words quickly and accurately. We want students to be meaning seekers who are able to read words quickly, easily, and meaningfully.

3. Fluency develops from practice (National Reading Panel, 2000). A review of in-school voluntary reading programs (SSR, self-selected reading, and intensive reading) was conducted by Krashen (2004) to summarize the effects of such programs on tests of reading comprehension. He found that students in such programs did "as well or better than students who were engaged in traditional programs" (Krashen, 2004, p. 2). There is no substitute for an abundance of reading from a wide variety of printed materials. Commenting on independent reading, Samuels (2006) notes that "the amount of time spent in independent reading should match the student's reading ability. For higher ability readers, 40 minutes of independent reading proved to be effective. However, for the lower ability readers, 15 minutes of independent reading proved effective" (p. 33). In another study, Kuhn (2004/2005) combined practice with wide reading to significantly improve the comprehension of struggling readers. In Part 2 of the book, we offer a range of activities to help students practice reading. Some of the methods involve individual reading, partner reading, sharing in small groups, and whole class activities. A key feature of the practice is multiple readings of the same text. Such rereadings help build both fluency and confidence.

4. Fluency is dependent on a variety of factors. The difficulty, complexity, and interest level of the materials used for instruction and practice impact fluency. Ideally, materials should be appropriate in difficulty and of interest to students. Helpful sources of leveled books for use in kindergarten through sixth grade have been developed by Fountas and Pinnell (2000, 2001) and Pinnell and Fountas (2002). The most critical factor in interventions for struggling readers is matching them with reading materials that "they can actually read with a high level of accuracy, fluency, and comprehension" (Allington, 2009, p. 45).

5. Fluency interventions can be differentiated based on student need. Current practices to increase or improve fluency often reflect the one-size-fits-all mentality. Instead, we would like you to use what you know or learn about your students to consider targeting particular strategies to specific students. This is often referred to as responsive instruction or intervention.

   You have probably already employed different interventions to help students in word identification. For example, if three students have difficulty with word recognition, one student may need to increase sight vocabulary, another student may need instruction in the sounds associated with selected vowels, and a third student may need to be taught how to use prefixes and suffixes along with base words to help identify longer words.

Students need to understand that the goal of reading is the construction of meaning.

In Part 2, we provide a similar approach for fluency. You may be able to focus your instruction on strategies that may be especially helpful to a particular student or to a small group of students. Some strategies might also be used with the entire class.

6. Fluency can be improved by high-quality teaching. Modeling and thinking out loud are two of the explicit actions you can take to help students become fluent readers. You can model fluent reading and take time to discuss what makes reading fluent. Teaching phrasing and providing guided practice will also help remove some of the mystery of fluency. In short, be ready to be explicit with your instruction when it is necessary. Systematic teaching will not leave the skill of fluency to chance. Allington (2009, p. 34) has argued that many "fluency problems are instructionally induced and instructionally maintained." Perhaps you can critically examine your teaching behaviors to identify those that may contribute to students' dysfluency in reading. In the words of Teale and Shanahan (2001, p. 8), "there are few positive changes as straightforward and potentially productive as an appropriate focus on fluency. It is time for us to stop ignoring the essential and to teach fluency as a regular part of our reading programs." That teaching should be of the highest quality.

Systematic teaching will include the skill of fluency.

15. What Is the Purpose of Fluency Instruction?

The basic purpose of fluency instruction is to make it as easy as possible for students to decode and comprehend text. Word-by-word reading, poor phrasing, and lack of expression all diminish students' ability to understand text. While inefficiency in identifying words is the most important factor in fluency for students who struggle in reading (Torgesen, 2004), data from the National Assessment of Educational Progress revealed that approximately three-quarters of fourth graders tested could read with sufficient accuracy, but only sixy-one percent could read fluently (Daane, Campbell, Grigg, Goodman, & Oranje, 2005). Fluency, then, is not ensured if students can recognize words automatically. What is needed for many students is an intentional approach to fluency as a core element in the reading program. Part 2 of this book offers a number of strategies, activities, and resources that will help you provide high-quality fluency instruction.

A key feature of fluency practice is multiple readings of text.

PART 2

Foundational Principles of Fluency Instruction; Evidence-Based Strategies, Activities, and Resources

FIGURE 2.1

Foundational Principles of Fluency Instruction

This part of the book contains instructional principles, strategies, activities, and resources to help students become fluent readers. Here we provide five foundational principles to guide your teaching. See Figure 2.1.

1. Match Students' Reading Abilities to Appropriate Materials for Instruction

Topping (2006) identifies the management of text difficulty as an important predisposing factor facilitating the development of fluency. To help match students' reading levels to appropriate instructional materials, you might want to use an informal reading inventory like the *Basic Reading Inventory* (Johns, Elish-Piper, & Johns, 2017). Three reading levels can be determined: independent, instructional, and frustration. The independent level is characterized by highly accurate word recognition (99% accuracy), comprehension (90%), and fluency. This would be the level for independent reading and Read and Relax (see page 102). Allington (2009) suggests that any text that cannot be read with 99% accuracy is probably too difficult for fostering fluency.

The instructional level is characterized by mostly accurate word recognition (95% or better) and comprehension (75%). The instructional level is where instruction is likely to be most effective so long as there is an appropriate match between a student's reading level and the materials used for instruction or practice. Instruction in fluency is usually done with materials that are at or near the student's instructional level. If guided reading is used, materials should be selected that are at their instructional level. According to Burns (2001), a critical foundation of guided reading is that students read materials at their respective instructional levels. However, Opitz and Ford (2001) point out that matching texts with students can be challenging because the interaction among texts, readers, and reading contexts is highly complex and involves a number of variables. Likewise, Allington (2006) asserts that many students who exhibit dysfluent reading are products of poorly designed instructional environments. Their dysfluency is "a signal that they have been routinely given the wrong texts, texts that are too difficult" (p. 101). Your goal should be to instruct students in materials at their instructional levels.

Gunning (2011) advises adhering to the 95 to 98 percent word recognition standard. He reflected on his own experiences teaching below this standard noting, "if six or more words out of every hundred were unknown, students' reading was slow and labored" (p. 126). It is important to ensure reading materials align with students' reading levels as it can greatly impact their fluency. In fact, one experimental study found that struggling readers instructed in materials at their reading level made significantly greater gains in fluency than students who used grade-level materials (O'Connor, Bell, Harty, Larkin, Sacker, & Zigmond, 2002).

The third reading level, frustration, is characterized by 90% word recognition and 50% comprehension. Materials at this level are not generally appropriate for instruction and should be avoided. Unfortunately, too many students are asked to read materials at their frustration level. When this situation occurs, students are likely to exhibit lack of expression in oral reading, lip movement in silent reading, finger pointing, and difficulty in pronouncing words. Teachers observe that students become more impatient, disruptive, and reliant on directions from others.

The bottom line: For fluency development, use instructional materials where students can recognize 95% or more of the words and practice with materials where students know 99% of the words.

2. Model Oral Reading

Daily oral reading to students should be an integral part of the instructional program. Many professionals agree that reading orally to students:

- stimulates language development.
- shows that reading is pleasurable.
- demonstrates that print is meaningful.
- fosters an interest in printed materials.
- stimulates students to react to what is read.
- helps develop favorable attitudes toward reading.
- encourages students to listen actively.
- serves as a model.
- builds rapport.
- helps broaden vocabulary knowledge.

With respect to fluency, students will hear you share how oral reading should sound. Phrasing, emphasis, and tone are some of the aspects of fluency that can be modeled through daily periods of reading aloud.

3. Provide Guided Oral Reading Opportunities

There are a number of guided oral reading procedures (e.g., radio reading, paired reading) in which teachers are typically involved, especially as these procedures are initially introduced and modeled. The impact of such teaching, modeling, and feedback results in student learning. The National Reading Panel (2000) concluded that such procedures had a consistent and positive impact on word recognition, fluency, and comprehension for a wide range of readers over a wide range of levels (i.e., first grade through college). Later in Part 2, we provide a number of ways you can provide repeated oral reading opportunities for students to improve fluency and overall reading achievement.

The current instructional focus on fluency in many schools is on speed and accuracy. This focus may predispose students to think that reading aloud fast and accurately is the goal, and understanding what is read is, at best, unimportant or an afterthought.

4. Offer Daily Opportunities for Students to Read Easy Materials Independently

The amount of time students spend in silent reading in the average classroom is limited. Silent reading in the typical primary school class is estimated at approximately 7 or 8 minutes per day, which is less than 10% of the total time devoted to reading. The National Reading Panel (2000) could neither confirm nor deny the effectiveness of sustained silent reading given the limited empirical research studies on this topic. That is, the National Reading Panel "did not find any evidence supporting the effectiveness of encouraging independent silent reading as a means of improving reading achievement" (p. 3-4). However, they do assert that sustained silent reading is not effective when used as the only type of reading instruction to increase students' reading fluency.

The National Reading Panel (2000) considered "all formal efforts to increase the amounts of independent or recreational reading" (p. 3-1) by students. Such reading should typically involve materials that are easy for the student. Materials at the student's easy or independent level are read with a high degree of accuracy (98% or more; Gunning 2011) and comprehension (Johns, Elish-Piper, & Johns, 2017). Providing a daily period for students to read materials independently may:

- increase reading achievement.
- boost motivation and engagement for reading.
- provide the means to practice and develop effective reading skills and strategies.
- foster a desire to read outside of school.
- promote a sense of agency or independence.
- encourage students to become lifelong learners (Allington, 2014; Block & Mangieri, 2002; Cunningham & Stanovich, 1998; Gardiner, 2005; Reutzel & Juth, 2014).

Krashen (2004) summarized the impact of in-school voluntary reading programs (SSR, intensive reading, and self-selected reading) on tests of reading comprehension. He found that "in 51 out of 54 comparisons (94%), readers do as well or better than students who were engaged in traditional programs" (p. 2). In our professional judgment, therefore, voluntary reading is worthwhile, even if much of the evidence is correlational. We encourage increased voluntary reading in classrooms.

It is generally acknowledged that there are vast differences in the volume of reading among struggling and achieving readers (Guthrie, 2004). You can help your students who struggle by increasing the amount of time they are given to read materials where they know 99% of the words and can consolidate the skills and abilities that will help them become proficient readers.

5. Support English Learners

Both English Learners (ELs) and Emergent Bilinguals (EBs) are terms currently used in the field to describe students who speak a language other than English at home. We will simply use the term English Learner or EL in this book. English Learners come to our schools with a wide range of proficiencies in language, subject matter knowledge, varying educational backgrounds, and school expectations. Some students have had rich educational experiences before coming to the United States, while others have very limited, if any, formal schooling.

These students have the highest risk for educational failure. Due to these many differences, there is no one-size-fits-all template for instructing ELs. The following are some tips to help you maximize instructional opportunities for your ELs.

1. Have clearly focused objectives defined, displayed, and reviewed.
2. Connect content to student experiences.
3. Target vocabulary development.
4. Provide daily instruction in oral language and opportunities to practice.
5. Restate or rephrase student responses to model proficient English usage and focus on students' meaning rather than on their grammar usage.
6. Face students when speaking; speak clearly with frequent pauses.
7. Minimize the use of idioms.
8. Increase wait time.

In addition, consider using the following, adapted from Short and Echevarria (2004), to enhance the teaching/learning experience.

- cooperative learning
- visual demonstrations, hands-on manipulatives, and realia (real life objects, many collected by students)
- adapted text and supplementary materials
- highlighted text
- recorded text
- graphic organizers and visuals
- language experience approach (writing down and rereading what students say)

Keep in mind that children learn to speak English most effectively when they are actively involved in oral language practice and are provided with multiple opportunities to communicate with each other. However, engaging in meaningful social interactions with students and teachers in the classroom can be particularly challenging for ELs if they do not share the same language and culture with those individuals (Monobe, Bintz, & McTeer, 2017). This can lead to ELs feeling isolated from their peers (Genishi & Dyson, 2009), and can ultimately inhibit their academic performance. Two ways to target this challenge are to 1) implement instructional strategies that are inclusive and support ELs' engagement in academic tasks in the classroom, and 2) boost ELs' motivation and self-efficacy (Monobe et al., 2017). Doing so may lead to increased English proficiency for ELs. Monobe and colleagues (2017) suggest using repeated readings, which increases students' oral fluency, and whole-class repeated reading, which not only improves student decoding and fluency skills, but also supports an environment where ELs can comfortably engage in social learning.

Building Blocks for Fluency

Developing a Base of Language, Sounds, and Words

Teacher Read Alouds

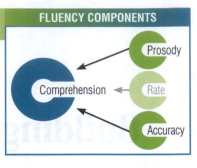

FLUENCY COMPONENTS

Prosody
Comprehension
Rate
Accuracy

Materials
- Various

Use
- Whole Group
- Small Group

Description

Being read to is widely considered to be a critical factor in becoming a successful reader (Routman, 2000). Reading aloud as little as fifteen minutes per day exposes children to the pleasure of reading and to a variety of books and genres. Research has established that effective read alouds contribute to comprehension development (Santoro, Chard, Howard, & Baker, 2008). It also expands students' experiential base and develops positive attitudes towards reading in general. While reading aloud is sometimes considered most appropriate for primary-grade students, reading aloud is an excellent and appropriate activity for students of all ages. We believe that reading aloud to students is a critical building block for fluency. On the following page are suggested read alouds. Be sure to include selections from both narrative and informational sources in read-aloud experiences for your students. Before reading a book to students, read it yourself to confirm that it is appropriate and to check for elements that might challenge students' understanding. Reading aloud should be accompanied by prereading and post-reading discussion (Gunning, 2000). For additional read-aloud suggestions, see Santoro, Chard, Howard, and Baker (2008), Sullivan (2004) and the Indiana Library Federation (2001).

Tips for Reading Aloud

1. Preview the selection before reading it aloud to students.
2. Introduce the read-aloud selection by displaying the text, discussing the title and author, and inviting students to make predictions about the selection's content.
3. During reading, hold the text so that students can see any illustrations. Use your voice to convey the emotions suggested by the text and to highlight any important information. Stop periodically to clarify any words or concepts that may be unfamiliar to students and encourage students to predict what will happen next. Also, invite students to comment on or make a personal connection to the text.
4. After reading, invite students to respond to the text, make connections to their own lives or to topics related to the classroom, and discuss how their predictions changed as they listened.

Following is a list of some favorite read-aloud books. While all are designated for a specific grade range, some of them may be used across several grade levels. For example, *Charlotte's Web* is a favorite for a wide range of ages, and *The Tale of Despereaux* is enjoyed by primary-grade as well as intermediate-grade students.

Read-Aloud Books

Grades K–1

Brett, Jan. *The Mitten.*
Cannon, Janell. *Stellaluna.*
dePaola, Tomie. *Strega Nona.*
Duke, Kate. *Aunt Isabel Tells a Good One.*
Fleming, Denise. *In the Tall, Tall Grass.*
Freeman, Don. *Corduroy.*
Henkes, Kevin. *Wemberly Worried.*
Katz, Alan. *Take Me Out to the Ballgame and Other Silly Dilly Songs.*
Klassen, Jon. *This is Not My Hat.*
Lester, Helen. *Hooway for Wodney Wat.*
Litwin, Eric. *Pete the Cat: I Love my White Shoes.*
Martin, Bill. *Brown Bear, Brown Bear, What Do You See?*
Mayer, Mercer. *There's a Nightmare in my Closet.*
Numeroff, Laura Joffe. *If You Give a Mouse a Cookie.*
Rosen, Michael. *We're Going on a Bear Hunt.*
Rubin, Adam. *Dragons Love Tacos.*
Sendak, Maurice. *Where the Wild Things Are.*
Shannon, David. *No, David!*
Viorst, Judith. *Alexander and the Terrible, Horrible, No Good, Very Bad Day.*
Waber, Bernard. *Ira Sleeps Over.*
Willems, Mo. *There is a Bird on Your Head.*
White, E. B. *Charlotte's Web.*
Wood, Audrey. *The Napping House.*
Various. *In Daddy's Arms I am Tall: African Americans Celebrating Fathers.*

Grades 2–3

Allard, Harry. *Miss Nelson Is Missing.*
Avi. *Finding Providence: The Story of Roger Williams.*
Barnes, Derrick. *Crown: An Ode to the Fresh Cut.*
Beaty, Daniel. *Knock, Knock: My Dad's Dream for Me.*
Cooney, Barbara. *Eleanor.*
Dahl, Roald. *James and the Giant Peach.*
Dicamillo, Kate. *The Tale of Despereaux.*
Fleischman, Sid. *The Whipping Boy.*
Ganeri, Anita. *Eruption! The Story of Volcanoes.*
Gibbons, Gail. *Spiders.*
Giff, Patricia Reilly. *The Beast in Mrs. Rooney's Room.*
Hoffman, Mary. *Amazing Grace.*
Kinney, Jeff. *Diary of a Wimpy Kid.*
Lovell, Patty. *Stand Tall, Molly Lou Melon.*
Robinson, Barbara. *The Best School Year Ever.*
Sachar, Louis. *Sideways Stories from Wayside School.*
VanAllsburg, Chris. *Polar Express.*
Winthrop, Elizabeth. *The Castle in the Attic.*
Yolen, Jane. *Owl Moon.*

Grades 4–6

Applegate, Katherine. *The One and Only Ivan.*
Banks, Lynn Reid. *The Indian in the Cupboard.*
Black, Wallace B. and Blashfield, Jean F. *Pearl Harbor!*
Christie, R. Gregory & Nelson, Vaunda Micheaux. *Bad News for Outlaws: The Remarkable Life of Bass Reeves, Deputy U.S. Marshall*
Cleary, Beverly. *Dear Mr. Henshaw.*
Clements, Andrew. *Frindl.*
Creech, Sharon. *Love that Dog.*
Curtis, Christopher Paul. *Bud, Not Buddy.*
Cooper, Susan. *Dark is Rising.*
Dicamillo, Kate. *Because of Winn Dixie.*
Gardiner, John. *Stone Fox.*
Levine, Ellen. *Henry's Freedom Box.*
Palacio, R.J. *Wonder*
Parks, Rosa (with James Haskins). *Rosa Parks: My Story.*
Paterson, Katherine. *Bridge to Terabithia.*
Peck, Richard. *Fair Weather.*
Pennypacker, Sara. *Clementine.*
Rathmann, Peggy. *Ruby the Copycat.*
Rawls, Wilson. *Where the Red Fern Grows.*
Reynold, Jason. *As Brave As You.*
Sachar, Louis. *Holes.*
Scieszka, Jon and Smith, Lane. *Math Curse.*
Spinelli, Jerry. *Maniac Magee.*
Taylor, Mildred. *Roll of Thunder, Hear My Cry.*
Tsuchiya, Yukio. *Faithful Elephants.*
Twain, Mark. *Tom Sawyer.*

Grades 7–8

Adler, David A. *The Babe and I.*
Bunting, Eve. *Terrible Thing: An Allegory of the Holocaust.*
Curtis, Christopher Paul. *The Watsons Go to Birmingham.*
Clements, Andrew. *The Landry News.*
Cushman, Karen. *Catherine Called Birdy.*
Davis, Kenneth. *Don't Know Much About American History.*
Hiaasen, Carl. *Hoot.*
Hinton, S. E. *The Outsiders.*
Konigsburg, E. L. *Silent to the Bone.*
Lester, Julius. *From Slave Ship to Freedom Road.*
Lord, Cynthia. *Rules.*
Lowry, Lois. *The Giver.*
Neri, Greg. *Yummy: The Last Days of a Southside Shorty.*
Paulsen, Gary. *Hatchet.*
Polacco, Patricia. *The Bee Tree.*
Ryan, Pam Muñoz. *Esperanza Rising.*
Snicket, Lemony. *The Series of Unfortunate Events.*
Watson, Jesse Joshua & Neri, Greg. *Ghetto Cowboy.*
Watson, Renée. *Piecing Me Together.*
Woodson, Jacqueline. *Brown Girl Dreaming.*
Woodson, Jacqueline. *Hush.*
Yolen, Jane. *Girl in a Cage.*

Language Experience

Prosody

Comprehension ← Rate

Accuracy

Materials

- Chart paper or a surface board

Use

- Whole Group
- Small Group

Description

The Language Experience approach involves writing down what students say, then reading and rereading it with them to develop knowledge of letter-sound associations, sight words, prosody, and language (Mallon & Berglund, 1984; Strickland, Ganske, & Monroe, 2002). Stories created in this manner are usually placed in a prominent location in the classroom or bound into class books to be used as text material for independent reading. Students can generally read language experience stories successfully because they have participated in their development. Because the text reflects the language, culture, and experiences of the students, lessons using these materials are especially appropriate for English Learners (Herrell, 2000).

Procedure

1. Gather students near an easel with chart paper or a surface board. Provide an experience or discuss something that is of current interest to students, such as a field trip, holiday, recent event, classroom pet, or picture.

2. As students describe the experience or topic, encourage them to use complete sentences. Repeat what is said and write it down, saying each word as you write it. Include the speaker's name as in the following example.

> Mark said, "The guinea pig was sleeping this morning."

3. After writing each sentence, read it aloud smoothly and expressively. Ask the speaker, "Is this what you meant to say? Did I write it the way you said it?" Make changes as needed. Invite students to read the sentence with you.

4. Invite students to dictate additional sentences. Reread them to and with students. Additional comments about the guinea pig might be as follows.

> Emily said, "I hope it is OK."
> Erica added, "I had a guinea pig once and it slept during the day, too."
> Jerry said, "I don't think we should worry. He is probably OK."
> Tyrone said, "Let's look at him again tomorrow and see if he is asleep again."
> "If he is, I think we will feel better," offered Shaunice.

5. When the story appears to be finished, read it to students, modeling good oral reading. Ask students to read along with you. Sweep your hand under the words as they are read.

6. Ask, "Is there anything else we should add? Have we written the story just the way we want it? Do you think someone who reads the story will understand our message?" This is an important time to emphasize that reading can be talk written down, and that the purpose of speaking and writing is to communicate a message.

7. On successive days, read the story chorally (see page 49) with students. Ask individual students to choose a sentence or sentences to read aloud. If a student has difficulty with a word, provide assistance. Celebrate when students read with appropriate speed, accuracy, and expression.

8. Post the story in a prominent place in the classroom or place it in a class book so that students can read and reread it independently. Invite students to add illustrations to enhance meaning and add interest for the reader.

Using a Student's Story to Develop Fluency
© ESB Professional/Shutterstock.com

Phonemic Awareness

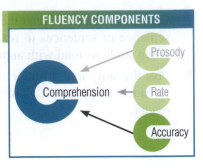

FLUENCY COMPONENTS

Comprehension — Prosody, Rate, Accuracy

Materials
- Various

Use
- Whole Group
- Small Group
- Individual

Description

Phonological and phonemic awareness have been recognized as important factors in learning to read (National Reading Panel, 2000). Phonological awareness involves the ability to hear syllables, onsets, and rimes in spoken words. Phonemic awareness is one aspect of phonological awareness (Yopp & Yopp, 2000). Phonemic awareness refers to the ability to notice, think about, and work with the individual sounds (phonemes) in spoken words (Armbruster, Lehr, & Osborn, 2001). When students begin to associate these spoken sounds with the letters, they are linking their phonemic knowledge to their written form, the grapheme. This becomes phonics. Phonics is the understanding of how sounds relate to letters and how our written language system works (Armbruster, Lehr, & Osborn, 2001). To put it concisely, phonological awareness and phonemic awareness in themselves do not involve print; phonics does. Because of its common use in the literature and in professional discussions, the term phonemic awareness will be used.

Why Phonemic Awareness Is Important

Phonemic awareness is a potent predictor of success in learning to read (Baker, Beattie, Nelson, & Turtura, 2018; NELP, 2008; National Reading Panel, 2000) and its absence predicts the likelihood of failure in learning to read (Adams, 1990). Helping students become aware of the phoneme, the smallest unit of sound in speech, leads to the development of an understanding of the alphabetic principle, an important prerequisite to being able to decode written words. Several studies have found that combining phonemic awareness activities with letter-sound instruction can be especially supportive of students' developing understanding of the alphabetic principle (NELP, 2008; National Reading Panel, 2000).

Developmental Progression

The following progression of skills, suggested by Ehri, Nunes, Willows, Schuster, Yaghoub-Zadeh, and Shanahan (2001) and Blachman (2000), shows how students move from early to deep awareness of phonemes on their way to becoming skilled readers.

Students who are becoming phonemically aware increasingly demonstrate the ability to perform the eleven tasks described on the next page.

1. **Recognize that sentences are composed of individual words.** (How many words are in this sentence? The dog went in his house. Clap each word.)
2. **Recognize and produce rhyming words.** (Do these words rhyme? Can, fan, van. Can you say another word that rhymes with these words?)
3. **Recognize and produce syllables.** (How many syllables do you hear in this word? Peanut. Clap each syllable. Can you say another two-syllable word? Clap each syllable.)
4. **Recognize and produce onsets and rimes.** (How are these words alike? Flake, flip, flat? Can you say another word that begins with /fl/? How are ride, hide, side alike? Can you think of another word that ends with /ide/?)
5. **Recognize and produce words with the same initial sound.** (What sound do you hear at the beginning of these words? Paper, pen, pencil. Can you say another word that starts with the /p/ sound?)
6. **Recognize and produce words with the same ending sound.** (What sound do you hear at the end of these words? Pen, can, fun. Can you say another word that ends with the /n/ sound?)
7. **Recognize oddity.** (Which word is not like the others? Bag, nine, beach, bat.)
8. **Blend individual phonemes to make a word.** (What word do we have when we put these sounds together c/a/t?)
9. **Segment words into their individual sounds.** (What sounds do you hear in up?)
10. **Substitute or add phonemes to a word.** (What word would we have if we added an /m/ to eat? What word would we have if we changed the /m/ to /b/? If we changed the /t/ to /m/? If we added an /s/ at the end?)
11. **Recognize and produce words with one phoneme deleted.** (What word would we have if we left the /t/ off the end of seat?)

Considerations

It is important to remember that phonemic awareness instruction is only one part of a rich literacy program. Students can develop sensitivity to the sound structure of language through the use of songs, chants, and word play activities. When phonemic awareness skills are specifically taught, it may be important to teach one skill at a time and demonstrate how the skill applies to reading or spelling (Ehri et al., 2001). Instruction should generally consist of no more than twenty hours over the course of the school year, with individual sessions consisting of thirty minutes or less (Ehri et al., 2001; Stanovich, 1993).

Basic Sight Vocabulary

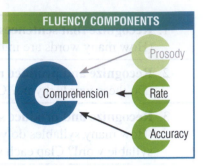

FLUENCY COMPONENTS

Materials

- Word Cards
- Phrases
- Word Lists

Use

- Small Group
- Partner

Description

Reading fluency problems of students who struggle in reading occur primarily because of "their difficulties forming large vocabularies of words that they can recognize 'by sight' or at a single glance" (Torgesen & Hudson, 2006, p. 152). There are about 200 basic sight words that occur over and over in the English language (Johns, 1976). These words can comprise over 60% of the words used in beginning reading materials and over 50% of the words used in materials in the upper grades and beyond (including materials read by adults). This explains why the words are commonly referred to as *basic, high-frequency,* or *function* words. Students need to know these words automatically if they are to become fluent readers. Such words are a necessary, but not sufficient, condition for efficient reading. They are often difficult for students to learn because many of the words look similar, are abstract, and are not considered "regular" in pronunciation. Two basic word lists are provided for your use. The Revised Dolch List (Johns, 1976) and High-Frequency Nouns (Johns, 1975) can be found on page 34 and page 35 respectively. They provide words for teaching and practice. Below are some tips for teaching and practicing basic sight words. Several additional strategies are offered by Johns and Lenski (2019).

Ideas for Instruction and Practice

1. **Create Instructional Materials.** Use words from the Revised Dolch List (Figure 2.2) and High-Frequency Nouns (Figure 2.3) to create phrases, sentences, and short stories that students can read and reread to learn the words and gain confidence. You might want to invite older students to use the lists to prepare materials that can be used by their peers or younger students in a different grade. The phrases and sentences can be written on cards. The stories can be bound into simple little books and illustrated by the student who authored the book or the student who reads the book. Provide repeated opportunities for students to read the materials individually, with partners, and at home. Stress the need to read accurately with expression. Model as needed. Examples are shown below. Phrases using high-frequency words can be found on pages 36–38 (Figure 2.4).

Phrases

by the road
over by the school

Sentences

What time of the year is it?
Her work was done very well.
That thing has two heads!

Short Story (A little book with a line on each page)

My Father
I have a father.
He is a good man.
He works in a big city.
He gives me money.
Next year, he will get a new blue car.
It is time for me to go home from school.
My father will be at home.
He is going to get me a little dog.
The dog will be a good friend.
My father and I will play with him.
What should I call my dog?

2. **Use Pattern Books.** Select a particular pattern book that contains the word or words you want to help students learn or practice. There are many pattern books, and a large listing of such books can be found in Johns and Lenski (2010). Read the book aloud to students and, if possible, use a big book version so students can follow along. Reread the book, inviting students to read along, as they are able. You may wish to point to each word as it is read. Provide opportunities for students to take turns reading the book to each other. Later, you could prepare sentence strips with words from the pattern book and invite students to read the text from the sentence strips. The sentence strips could be cut up, and students could rearrange the words in order and read the sentence. Stress the need for meaningful phrasing and attention to punctuation. Older students could be invited to share some of the pattern books with younger students, thus helping to develop reader confidence.

3. **Teach Words Explicitly.** Students may persistently misread some of the basic sight words. Note the troublesome words and develop lessons to teach the words. Write the word on the board; students can write the word on a card. Chant the word. Then spell the word and say it as a class two or three times (e.g., w-e-n-t, went, w-e-n-t, went, w-e-n-t, went). Write several sentences on the board with a blank space for the word being learned. Invite students to read the sentence silently and then ask a volunteer to print the missing words in the sentence. Have the sentence read aloud, using good phrasing and expression. You should also model for students as needed. A few examples are shared below.

Joann and Cheyenne _____ to the soccer game.

I _____ to see my friend, Javon.

I hit the ball and it _____ about ten feet!

Do you know where she _____?

Students can also be invited to find the troublesome words in materials they read. Because basic sight words appear frequently, help students understand that knowing such words will enable them to read more quickly and easily.

Revised Dolch List

a	could	he	might	same	told
about	cut	heard	more	saw	too
across	did	help	most	say	took
after	didn't	her	much	see	toward
again	do	here	must	she	try
all	does	high	my	short	turn
always	done	him	near	should	two
am	don't	his	need	show	under
an	down	hold	never	six	up
and	draw	hot	next	small	upon
another	eat	how	new	so	us
any	enough	I	no	some	use
are	even	I'm	not	soon	very
around	every	if	now	start	walk
as	far	in	of	still	want
ask	fast	into	off	stop	warm
at	find	is	oh	take	was
away	first	it	old	tell	we
be	five	its	on	ten	well
because	for	just	once	than	went
been	found	keep	one	that	were
before	four	kind	only	the	what
began	from	know	open	their	when
best	full	last	or	them	where
better	gave	leave	other	then	which
big	get	left	our	there	while
black	give	let	out	these	white
blue	go	light	over	they	who
both	going	like	own	think	why
bring	gone	little	play	this	will
but	good	long	put	those	with
by	got	look	ran	thought	work
call	green	made	read	three	would
came	grow	make	red	through	yes
can	had	many	right	to	yet
close	hard	may	round	today	you
cold	has	me	run	together	your
come	have	mean	said		

FIGURE 2.2

The rationale and research for this list are described in Johns, J. L. (1976). Updating the Dolch basic sight vocabulary. *Reading Horizons, 16*, 104–111.

From Melanie Walski, Peet Smith, Jerry L. Johns, and Roberta L. Berglund, *Fluency: Questions, Answers, and Evidence-Based Strategies* (5th ed.). Copyright © 2020 Kendall Hunt Publishing Company. May be reproduced for noncommercial educational purposes.

High-Frequency Nouns

air	group	people
back	hand	place
book	head	road
boy	home	room
car	house	school
children	man	side
city	men	table
day	money	thing
dog	morning	time
door	mother	top
eye	Mr.	town
face	Mrs.	tree
father	name	water
feet	night	way
friend	nothing	year
girl		

FIGURE 2.3

The development of this list is described in Johns, J. L. (1975). Dolch list of common nouns—A comparison. *The Reading Teacher, 28,* 338–340.

Fast Phrases

a big green tree	been going to play	didn't know which one	gave some away
about that girl	before she said	do go to town	get one through
across her face	began to hold	does keep his dog	give him one
after this morning	best place	done with that	go with them
again today	better book	don't leave now	going away
all around my house	big green house	down and up	gone for good
always going together	long black road	draw some people	good enough for me
I am not	cold blue water	eat in the morning	got close to it
an old school	both good and bad	enough to keep	green and blue
father and mother	bring a friend	even though	grow up
another friend	but then	every little thing	had to help her
any old place	by the tree	far away	hard to do
are going	to call him	fast enough for me	has a cold
around the room	came into the room	find out which one	have to go
as he heard	can go together	first thing	he and she
ask to help	close the door	high five	heard a dog
at another city	cold water	not for long	help find out
going away	come together	found out	her own town
over here	be open	could read a book	four more

FIGURE 2.4

(continued)

From Melanie Walski, Peet Smith, Jerry L. Johns, and Roberta L. Berglund, *Fluency: Questions, Answers, and Evidence-Based Strategies* (5th ed.). Copyright © 2020 Kendall Hunt Publishing Company. May be reproduced for noncommercial educational purposes.

Fast Phrases

high up	because he heard her	cut through it	from here to there
with him	did look away	full of light	his small feet
hold my hand	make another friend	old red school	see a tree
hot enough for me	she and I	how long	many more
on top of that	short walk around	too much help	may it be
once there was	should have been	why I'm small	find me first
one of those feet	show how big	if I can	big and mean
only two more	five or six	in its house	might leave now
open the right one	small enough to	into the road	more than that
or you might not	so short that	is enough	most of all
other than that	some of that	before it was	much more than that
our little children	group	its own place	out the door
soon enough	just enough	must have been	over the tree
start to go	keep near	my new dog	our own house
still more than	what kind of thing	near the door	play with you
to stop	know how to read	need to go	put that away
some more	last one out	never tell	ran from me
to tell me	leave again	next one	read with
ten more than that	left or right	new day	red and black

FIGURE 2.4

(continued)

Fast Phrases

not more than this	let it go	no one around	right down there
while they play	light and fast	not now	his round face
the big thing	like any other	now we go	run away
their own home	little green me	one of those	said to me
not all of them	long gone	off the road	same as her
then there was	look around	oh stop	saw an eye
over there	made a friend	say nothing	these two people
took a car	they should start	very long road	your white house
toward the town	think about	to walk with me	try to run
turn around	this red table	want to go	two or three
under the table	those good children	a warm day	up and out
upon the door	was well done	with us	to use it
thought to leave	as we go	white and black	which one
three more than that	well enough	why both can go	will go away
went around	with both of them	work every day	through an old door
were never so small	would like to go	yes, there is	yet another one
you and she	to the town	what once was	before today
when we walk	together again	where you go	told to do

FIGURE 2.4

Word Identification

Materials

- Various

Use

- Whole Group
- Small Group

Prosody

Comprehension

Rate

Accuracy

Description

When students do not know words at sight (automatically), they need strategies for identifying such words. Often, these strategies are referred to as decoding strategies. Some of the most common decoding strategies are phonics, word patterns or phonograms, structural analysis (inflected endings like *s, es, ing*, and *ly*, compound words, prefixes, suffixes) and context (the words near the unknown word). Numerous books have information and teaching strategies for decoding (Fox, 2007; Johns & Lenski, 2019). For effective strategy instruction, intentional (explicit) teaching is necessary. A consistent finding of research is that "word identification development is involved in improving comprehension" (Breznitz, 2006, p. 43). The following strategies should strengthen students' word identification strategies.

Phonics Instruction and Practice

Phonics gives students a means to associate sounds with letters and letter combinations so they can pronounce a word not known at sight. The 26 letters in the English alphabet can represent over 40 sounds or phonemes. Some of the phonic elements commonly taught include initial consonants, final consonants, consonant digraphs, long vowel sounds, and short vowel sounds.

1. **Synthetic (Explicit) Phonics.** Directly teach students the name of the letter and the sound associated with it. Begin with initial letter sounds. Teach additional letters and sounds. Then help students learn to blend the sounds to say a word (*kkk-aaa-ttt* is *cat*). Provide numerous opportunities to practice the sounds taught. For example, use oral sentences and have students identify the word that begins with a particular sound (e.g., Help me identify some words at a birthday party that begin with *kkk*).

2. **Analytic (Deductive) Phonics.** Begin with words that students have in their oral vocabularies that start with the same letter sound (e.g., *bbb*—Bianca, Benicio, Bill, Beth, bee, bat, ball). As students offer words, write the words on the board under an uppercase or lowercase *b*. Use pictures and objects to stimulate students' backgrounds. Once the words are listed, help students understand the notion that *b* represents the same sound at the beginning of each word. Be explicit in making the connection between the letter and the sound. You might run your hand along each word as you say it, emphasizing the initial sound. Then invite students to add additional words to the list. Practice by saying some words that begin and do not begin with the sound taught. Students should listen and raise their hands when the word begins with the sound that is being taught.

3. **Alphabet Phonics.** Use alphabet books to help students learn and identify specific sounds. Read a selected page aloud and tell students which words begin with a specific sound. Do the same thing with the same letter in another alphabet book. Have students help you identify the words that begin with the same sound. Then have students suggest other words. To help practice, students can make their own alphabet books, a page at a time, as letters and sounds are taught. Magazine illustrations and drawn pictures can be used to help illustrate the page.

Word Pattern (Phonograms) Instruction and Practice

Some words are made up of an onset and rime (*hill* = the onset *h* and the rime *-ill*). Another name for rimes is phonograms. Some of the rimes that can be taught for short vowel sounds are listed in the box below. Rimes for the long vowel sounds can be found in Johns and Lenski (2019).

-ab	-ack	-ad	-ag	-am	-amp	-an	-and	-ang	-ank	-ap	-ash	-atch	-eck	-ed	-eg	-ell
-ess	-est	-et	-ob	-ock	-od	-og	-ong	-op	-ot	-ib	-ick	-id	-ift	-ig	-ill	-im
-in	-ing	-ink	-ip	-ish	-it	-itch	-ub	-uck	-ud	-uff	-ug	-ull	-um	-ump	-un	-unch
-ung	-up	-ush														

1. **Nursery Rhymes and Poetry.** Select nursery rhymes or poetry that contain rhyming words (e.g., "Jack and Jill"). Tell students that some words rhyme (sound the same at the end). Then have students listen for rhyming words as you read "Jack and Jill." Invite sharing about the rhyme and ask students to identify words that rhyme. Write the words on the board under each other. Guide students as necessary. Then help students identify the rime (*-ill*) and help them see how they can use this word part to help identify other words with the same part (e.g., *bill, fill, pill, drill*). Provide additional practice by supplying additional initial sounds and having students add *-ill* to make new words (e.g., *will, mill, gill, still, spill, quill*). Once the words are identified, use pictures or simple words to help students understand any word meanings that may be unknown. Students can also be encouraged to relate the words to their lives.

2. **Phonogram Instruction.** Choose a word that contains an onset and rime (e.g., *hay*). Write a sentence on the board containing the word: *Cows eat hay*. Read the sentence and underline the *–ay* sound. Tell students that they can probably make other words that have an *–ay* sound. Model an example (If h-a-y spells *hay*, what do you think d-a-y spells?). Then write the new word on the board. Provide several additional examples, inviting students to tell you the new word (e.g., *jay, lay, pay, bay, ray, say, clay, play, tray, stay*). Then write sentences for each of the new words, clarifying meanings as needed. Introduce additional word patterns to help students learn more word patterns that can be used to help decode words.

3. **Making Words.** Many easy-to-use lessons in making words have been provided by Cunningham and Hall (2009) and Hall and Cunningham (2009) in a book series for students in grades K–4. These lessons have students use letter tiles or letter cards to make words. Using the letters for a rime (e.g., *-ine*) and additional letters (d, f, l, m, n, p, v), tell students that you can use *–ine* and make words by adding a letter to the rime. Model an example and then have students make words independently using their individual letters. Once all the words have been written on the board, point out the similar features and stress that this knowledge can be used to help decode unknown words that have a similar pattern. You may want to extend the lesson by encouraging students to see how many different words they can make using two or more of the letters in any combination. Have students work individually or with partners and write their new words on a sheet of paper. Be sure to correct misspelled words and clarify word meanings as needed.

Structural Analysis Instruction and Practice

The Literacy Dictionary (Harris & Hodges, 1995) defines structural analysis as "the identification of roots, affixes, compounds, hyphenated forms, inflected and derived endings, contractions, and in some cases, syllabication. Structural analysis is sometimes used as an aid to pronunciation or in combination with phonic analysis in word-analysis programs" (pp. 244–245). Obviously, there's a lot to structural analysis! We have chosen to provide some instructional assistance for inflected and derived endings (e.g., *s, es, ed, ly*), compound words, and roots with affixes (prefixes and suffixes). For further resources consult Fox (2014) and Johns and Lenski (2019).

1. **Inflected and Derived Endings.** Inflected and derived endings are the *s, es, ed, ly, ing* and other endings that can be added to a word. Younger students may have difficulty recognizing known words like *want* that have an *s, ed,* or *ing* added. Older students may have trouble identifying longer words like *agreement* because of the *ment*. To help students identify words with inflected endings, begin with a word that students know (e.g., fish, play, want, jump, laugh, record, help, end) and systematically model how you can identify word endings in an effort to identify the unknown word. Write *fishing* on the board and then think aloud to show students how you look for a known word with an ending. Identify the known word and then look at the ending. Underline the word and the ending. Pronounce each and then blend the two together to identify the word. Provide numerous examples to students, gradually increasing the difficulty. Then invite students to make new words adding inflected endings to words they already know (e.g., talk, talks, talked, talking).

2. **Compound Words.** Sometimes two smaller words are put together to make a longer word. Tell students that such words are called compound words. Write a sentence on the board that has a compound word (e.g., I got homesick when I went to camp.). Have students identify the longest word and tell them that it is a compound word. Then have students look for the smaller words to help them pronounce the longer word. Be explicit in helping students realize that when they are reading and they come across an unknown word, one strategy they can use is to look and see if it is made up of two smaller words. Provide additional compound words and see if students are able to identify them. Use the words in oral or written sentences and clarify word meaning as needed. The box below contains some compound words you may wish to use.

afternoon	everyone	pancake	airplane	everything	peanut
wristwatch	overboard	notebook	dragonfly	downstairs	wildlife
firecracker	playground	quarterback	fireplace	backbone	anybody
highchair	grasshopper	neighborhood	oatmeal	uphill	checkerboard
horseshoe	jellybean	motorcycle	whirlpool	rollerblade	strawberry
basketball	headset	fireworks	fingerprint	peppermint	turtleneck

3. **Prefixes, Suffixes, and Root Words.** To help students decode polysyllabic words, teach them to look for prefixes and suffixes attached to base or root words. For example, *replacement* is made up of a prefix *(re)*, base word *(place)*, and suffix *(ment)*. Sometimes students have little or no idea what to do in order to identify longer words like *replacement*. Write the word on the board and systematically show students the three parts. Identify each part using the appropriate terms. Tell students that when they come across a long word, they should look for a base or root word and a prefix and/or suffix. By separating the word into smaller parts, they can pronounce each part to try to say a word that they have heard before. Even if the word is not in their meaning vocabulary, they can use meanings for the prefixes and suffixes to arrive at a possible meaning for the word. Model several examples by thinking aloud. Then provide some longer words in sentences and have students try to use prefixes, roots, and suffixes to pronounce the word. Build greater mastery by teaching common meanings for common prefixes and suffixes. You may want to begin with the four most common prefixes that help provide meanings to approximately 66% of the English words that have prefixes (Armbruster, Lehr, & Osborn, 2001). These four prefixes are *un-, re-, in-,* and *dis-*. Additional words you might want to use for instruction in longer words are found in the box at the top of the next page.

replacement	nonliving	midnight	irresponsible	kindness	independence
hopeless	assistance	submarine	transportation	unfinished	valuable
composer	dishonest	expensive	inexpensive	indecent	indirect
ineligible	incorrect	inexact	unhappy	impractical	uncomfortable
illiterate	irreplaceable	uncovered	indivisible	inartistic	inequality
submarine	submerged	subnormal	subsonic	antifreeze	unsubscribe
unicycle	monocracy	monotone	biplane	biweekly	underlying
overflowed	undercooked	autograph	repay	retroactive	fearless
windowless	aimless	spotless	blameless	endless	guiltless
sweetness	thickness	greatness	sickness	nearness	tenderness

Context Instruction and Practice

Context refers to "information from the immediate textual setting that helps identify a word or word group" (Harris & Hodges, 1995, p. 44). For example, you can probably add additional words to this phrase: Fourscore and seven years ago, _____. That's a powerful context. Students can also use context to anticipate or identify a word: "Bow wow," said the big brown _____ (dog). Context clues and minimal phonic clues can often be used in tandem to identify words: I saw birds in the s_____. The initial letter in the missing word makes it clear that the correct word cannot be *tree* and that it is probably *sky*. Helping students use context along with letter sounds can be an effective strategy for identifying words.

1. **Oral Context.** Before using the context in texts to help students identify unknown words, engage students in oral activities. Tell students that they can use what they already know to help identify words. Begin with several examples that are easy for your students (e.g., "Meow," said the _____ (cat, kitten, kitty). Encourage students to explain why they have chosen certain words. Provide additional oral examples where multiple answers will make sense (e.g., I like to eat _____). Write words students offer on the board and help students evaluate whether each word makes sense. Ask students to evaluate additional words you suggest, offering some words (e.g., cars, tires, bolts) that do not make sense. Be sure students understand that they can use their knowledge about words in their reading to say words that make sense.

2. **Written Context.** Print a sentence on the board with a missing word. Have students read the sentence and predict what the word is likely to be. Use an initial sentence that will be easy for your students: I heard a _____ bark last night. Have students identify clues in the sentence that helped them to identify the word. Then provide a sentence where multiple words are possible: The cat sat by the _____. Invite students to share words and justify them. Offer some additional words that do and do not make sense. Add a letter clue in the sentence where the blank is and have students narrow their choices to one or two words: The cat sat by the d_____ (door, dog). Help students refine their predictions by offering additional letters until the word is known. Provide additional practice by offering clues for some words that are partially written on the board. Some possible examples are in the box below.

___ash (a name for money)	___eeth (you brush them)	___ent (name for a penny)
___ide (on the playground)	___ike (you ride on it)	___en (write with it)
___pple (a fruit)	___oice (can be loud or soft)	___ig (not small)
p___n (to fasten)	ch___k (used for writing)	s___n (bright yellow)
c___lf (baby cow)	c___e (holds ice cream)	f___ll (after summer)
hi___ (smaller than mountain)	cu___ (baby bear)	li___ (not dark)
di___ (worth ten cents)	bo___ (you read it)	ba___ (very small child)

3. **Context and Phonics.** Help students transfer the above strategies to their reading by using examples from enlarged texts and various reading selections in your curriculum. Select examples where a word in the text may be covered and easily identified because of the rich context. Then show the word to help students realize the power that context can have. Provide other examples where the context will permit more than one word to be suggested. Then gradually supply selected letters of the covered word to help students narrow their choices. Always encourage students to give reasons for their thinking before revealing the word. Sometimes students may be able to use the last line on a page and be able to predict the first word on the following page before turning the page. Help them realize that they are using context. Here's an actual example of a last line on a page from a book that one of us was reading: For each permissible combination of a word and suffix, write _____. Perhaps you also correctly predicted that *the* appeared at the top of the next page. You might also use examples from your own reading to help students realize the power of context and phonics for identifying words.

Identifying Context Clues

© Monkey Business Images/Shutterstock.com

Shared Reading

Modeling Fluent Oral Reading

Shared Book Experience

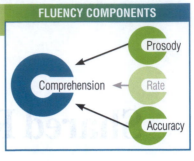

FLUENCY COMPONENTS

Prosody
Comprehension
Rate
Accuracy

Materials

- Enlarged text
- Small version of the enlarged text (optional)

Use

- Whole Group
- Small Group

Description

Sometimes viewed as a school version of the bedtime story, Shared Book Experience involves a teacher and a group of students sharing reading by listening to and rereading stories, rhymes, songs, and poems in an enjoyable manner (Berglund, 1988; Chung & Keckler, 2016; Scheffel & Booth, 2013). Shared Book Experience invites students into the reading process through the repeated sharing of materials that soon become favorites. Many insights about literacy can be taught from Shared Book Experiences. In order to increase visual intimacy with print, materials used for Shared Book Experiences are often enlarged books (big books) or text viewed using a document camera. Books and stories with repetitive language patterns or predictable story structures are especially useful for this experience.

Procedure

1. **Reread old favorites.** Begin with familiar rhymes, songs, poems, or chants that students know. These can be chosen either by you or by your students. Because these favorites are familiar to students, they can actively participate in the reading, particularly when there is repetitive text. For instance, for very young children, the chant, "Brown Bear, Brown Bear, What do you see?" is easily learned and repeated as the teacher reads and rereads this book (Martin, 1987). Point to the text as you read so that students can see the print, learn print conventions (left-right, top-bottom, front-back, punctuation, spaces, title), and note the connection between written and spoken language.

2. **Introduce a new story.** At least once a week, introduce a new story. Show the cover of the book and invite students to predict what the story may be about. Share the title, author, and illustrator with students and note if other books by the same author or illustrator were shared in previous readings.

3. **Read the story aloud.** Read the story all the way through, modeling good rate and expression. You may wish to stop at exciting points and allow students to check predictions and make new ones. The purpose of this segment of the lesson is to allow students to enjoy the story.

4. **Discuss the story.** Return to the predictions made as a class and invite students to confirm or revise them. Discuss the illustrations, characters, and favorite or exciting parts of the story to help students understand the meaning of the text. This is also a good time for students to be invited to make connections between the new story and any previous texts (text-to-text) or connections between the story and their own experiences (text-to-self) (Keene, 2008; Keene & Zimmermann, 1997).

5. **Reread the story aloud.** Invite students to join in the reading. Students may read a repetitive segment with you and add appropriate sound effects or hand gestures to enhance meaning.

6. **Make the text available for independent reading.** Put the enlarged text and/or smaller versions of the text in a reading corner or literacy center and encourage students to read it independently or with a friend.

7. **Use the text again for familiar rereadings and for teaching reading strategies.** During another Shared Book Experience, draw from the story previously read and discussed; after reading it, use the text to teach and practice the following:

- reading with expression and fluency
- sight vocabulary
- sound/symbol relationships
- word families
- effective reading strategies

8. **Encourage students to use the meaning of the story, how the language sounds, and letter-sound relationships to predict and self-correct their reading.** Use questions such as, "Does it make sense? Does it sound right? Does it look right?" to help students develop good fix-up strategies to use when the reading process breaks down.

Fluency practice might include inviting students to Echo Read the text with you (see page 48), discussing the use of typographic signals (Super Signals on page 53), practicing Phrased Reading (see page 57), or using Say It Like the Character (see page 88). Following the rereading of the text, it could be used again during Sustained Silent Reading (SSR) (see page 105) or Read and Relax (see page 102).

Evaluation

- Quality of predictions
- Text-to-text and text-to-self connections
- Accuracy of word identification
- Appropriate expression

Supporting a Student's Oral Reading

© Tracey Whiteside/Shutterstock.com

Echo Reading

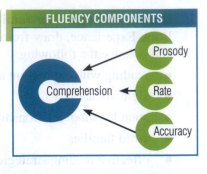

FLUENCY COMPONENTS

Prosody

Comprehension — Rate

Accuracy

Materials

- Reading selection

Use

- Whole Group
- Small Group

Description

Echo Reading involves modeling fluent reading for students and then encouraging them to reread, or echo, the same text, with support as needed. In Echo Reading, the student immediately echoes or imitates the performance of a more skilled reader. Doing so helps the student gain confidence in reading aloud, become proficient with material that might be too difficult for the student to read independently, and practice good phrasing and expression (Allington, 2001; Gillet, Temple, & Crawford, 2004).

Procedure

1. For students' initial experiences with echo reading, select fairly easy reading material. Stories with patterns or repeated phrases and poetry are excellent for beginning the activity. Students' language experience stories (see page 28) are also good sources for echo reading materials.

2. Read a phrase or sentence of the selection aloud. Call attention to any textual signals that help you determine the rate and expression you used. For the sentence, "'You're back!' Mama cried as her son walked through the door," you might say that the exclamation mark helped you know that you should read the sentence in an excited voice.

3. Reread the phrase or sentence and have students echo the same text immediately after you finish.

4. If students echo your reading effectively, mirroring your rate, accuracy, and expression, continue by modeling the next phrase or sentence. Then have students again echo your reading.

5. If students do not echo your reading effectively on the first try, model the phrase or sentence again and have students echo your reading again.

6. As students become proficient with easy materials, gradually move into more difficult materials.

Evaluation

- Accuracy of word identification
- Appropriate rate
- Expression similar to that modeled

Choral Reading

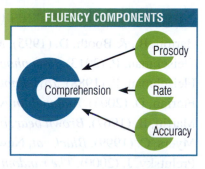
FLUENCY COMPONENTS

Prosody
Comprehension
Rate
Accuracy

Materials

- Reading selection

Use

- Whole Group
- Small Group

Description

Choral Reading involves students reading a text in unison. It helps build confidence and extend enjoyment of the reading process (Opitz & Rasinski, 2008). Repeated practice of choral reading materials helps to develop reading competence, nurtures collaboration among students, and helps students feel successful as readers.

Procedure

1. Select a text for use in the Choral Reading experience. Poetry or books with predictable story patterns, repeated phrases, or refrains work especially well. See the suggested resources that follow.

2. Provide copies of the text to each student in the group. Use a document camera to project the text or write the text on chart paper so that all can view it.

3. Read the text aloud to students, modeling fluent reading. Tell students why you chose to read it as you did. For example, were there punctuation marks that gave you clues? Perhaps there was bold print or underlining which gave you a clue about emphasis.

4. After your modeling, invite students to follow along and read with you. Practice reading together chorally several times.

5. You may wish to vary the Choral Reading experience by having students join in chorally for repeated refrains in the text. For instance, in the poem "The Jumblies" by Edward Lear in *Sing a Song of Popcorn* by deRegniers (1988), the refrain is one that students enjoy reading chorally, although the rest of the poem may be too difficult for them to read with fluency.

6. A further adaptation of Choral Reading is Antiphonal Reading (see page 51) where students are divided into groups, with each group reading its assigned part.

Evaluation

- Accuracy of word identification
- Appropriate rate
- Expression similar to that modeled

Suggested Resources (for Choral Reading)

Barton, B., & Booth, D. (1995). *Mother Goose goes to school*. Portland, ME: Stenhouse.

Fleischman, P. (2013). *I am phoenix: Poems for two voices*. New York: HarperCollins.

Fleischman, P. (1988). *Joyful noise: Poems for two voices*. New York: HarperCollins.

Florian, D. (2003). *Autumnblings*. New York: Greenwillow Books.

Martin, B. (1967). *Brown bear, brown bear, what do you see?* New York: Doubleday.

Myers, C. (1999). *Black cat*. New York: Scholastic.

Prelutsky, J. (2000). *The random house book of poetry for children*. New York: Random House.

Silverstein, S. (1974). *Where the sidewalk ends*. New York: HarperCollins.

Enjoying Choral Reading   Monkey Business Images/Shutterstock.com

Antiphonal Reading

FLUENCY COMPONENTS

Comprehension — Prosody, Rate, Accuracy

Materials

- Reading selection

Use

- Whole Group
- Small Group
- Partner

Description

Antiphonal Reading is an adaptation of choral reading. In Antiphonal Reading, students are usually divided into groups (Worthy & Broaddus, 2001/2002). Each group reads an assigned part—sometimes alternately, sometimes in unison. The manner of reading is cued by the placement of the text on the page. Usually Antiphonal Reading is done with poetry obtained from published sources or from materials students have created, but rhymes, limericks, and chants would also be suitable.

Procedure

1. Select the text to be read and make it visually accessible by providing copies for each student or by using a computer or document camera. Some resources are listed on the following page.

2. Explain to students the unique way this material is written, for instance, in two columns, indicating how it should be read.

3. Model for students how Antiphonal Reading in two parts is done by inviting an able student who is a risk-taker to be your partner. You begin by reading the first segment of print on the left side of the page. Your partner then reads the first segment of their part on the right side of the page. If both sides of the page contain the same print on the line, read that part in unison with your partner. Proceed through the entire selection, modeling good reading and the turn-taking that is involved in Antiphonal Reading. Point to the text as each of you read your respective parts so that the listeners understand the cues.

4. Now divide the students into two groups, with each group assigned either the left side or right side of the text.

5. Invite the groups to try reading the poem in the manner in which you and your partner have modeled it. Repeat the process several times, until students become proficient at reading their respective parts with fluency.

6. As a follow-up activity, you may wish to invite students to write poetry which follows the form introduced in Antiphonal Reading. On the next page is an example of a poem written in two parts by fourth-grade students.

The Titanic

Titanic	Titanic
	Hit an iceberg
Titanic	Titanic
Sank to the bottom of the sea	
Titanic	Titanic
Titanic	Titanic
Titanic	Titanic
	1,025 people died
700 people lived	
Titanic	Titanic
People went under water	
	To study the
Titanic	Titanic
	We want to know why
The Titanic sank	
Titanic	Titanic
Titanic	Titanic
Titanic	Titanic

by Rebecca and Mike

Evaluation

- Accuracy of word identification
- Appropriate rate
- Expression similar to that modeled

Suggested Resources

Fleischman, P. (2000). *Big talk: Poems for four voices*. Cambridge, MA: Candlewick.

Gerber, C. (2013). *Seeds, bees, butterflies, and more! (Poems for two voices)*. New York: Henry Holt.

Hoberman, M. A. (2007). *You read to me, I'll read to you: Very short scary tales to read together*. New York: Little, Brown.

Hoberman, M. A. (2001). *You read to me, I'll read to you: Very short stories to read together*. Boston: Little, Brown.

Panec, D. J. (2017). *Changing places*. Novato, CA: Treasure Bay.

Singer, M. (2010). *Mirror, mirror: A book of reversible verse*. New York: Scholastic.

Super Signals

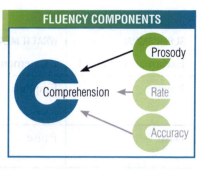

FLUENCY COMPONENTS

Prosody
Comprehension
Rate
Accuracy

Materials

- Various text selections
- Super Signals Chart (optional)

Use

- Whole Group
- Small Group

Description

Super Signals involves helping students look for and understand the typographic signals that are used to help convey the author's message. Signals such as bold or italic type, commas, exclamation marks, and type size are often clues to meaning that should be noted by the reader, particularly during oral reading.

Procedure

1. Select a text that contains signals you wish to help students understand, for example, bold or enlarged type, exclamation marks, or italicized type.

2. Use a big book or enlarge the passage with a document camera.

3. Read the selection aloud to the students, allowing them to see the text as you read. During the first reading, use no expression, pauses, or changes in pitch.

4. Reread the same passage aloud, using differing pitches, pauses, and expression as indicated by the text.

5. Discuss with students the differences in the two readings. Encourage them to explain why you changed your reading the second time. Ask them which reading helped them better understand the text.

6. Encourage students to note the signals in the text that helped you know when to pause, raise your voice, or stop. Note how using these signals enhances understanding of the text.

7. Provide students with text that contains some of the Super Signals you have just modeled. Ask them to first read the text silently and then to read it aloud, showing that they understand the signals. You may wish to use the following prompts to guide students as they read.

   - Make your voice go down when you see a period.
   - Make your voice go up when you see a question mark.
   - Change the volume of your voice or emphasize certain words or phrases when you see an exclamation point.
   - If you see parentheses, put in a short stop before and after them.
   - If there are quotation marks, read it like the person would say it.
   - When you see a comma, take a short breath.
   - Make your voice show the author's meaning.

8. Tell students to look for Super Signals in their reading and use these important clues to gain the author's meaning.

9. You may wish to create a classroom chart of Super Signals. Invite students to share Super Signals that they locate in their reading materials and note how these signals are used to convey meaning (Opitz & Rasinski, 1998). A sample chart follows on page 54.

SUPER SIGNAL	WHAT IT MEANS	EXAMPLE
Exclamation Mark !	Excitement	"Think! Think!"
Italics	Emphasis	"But I want more! And I want you to make it for me!" "Where did you get this?" he asked, showing her the gold.
Dash —	Pause	"You don't need them anymore—your people love you now."
Comma ,	Pause Cluster words between commas together as you read them.	And whenever the king started worrying about gold, she sent him on a goodwill trip throughout the countryside, which cheered him up.

Evaluation

- Increased awareness of typographic signals
- Appropriate use of typographic signals in text while reading

Noting Text Signals

Reading Punctuation

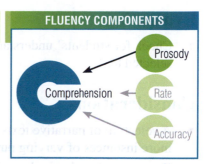

Materials

- Reading selection (a selection of narrative text is recommended)
- SmartBoard, DocCam, or Projector

Use

- Whole Group
- Small Group
- Partner

Description

Reading punctuation gives students the opportunity to learn about the comprehension cues and prosody clues that punctuation provides in text. Students who demonstrate good fluency skills employ pitch variability and distinctions that align with the text and use proper stress patterns when reading aloud (Schwanenflugel, Westmoreland, & Benjamin, 2015). Punctuation guides students to the appropriate uses of these variabilities and distinctions in pitch and stress patterns through their oral reading. For this activity, students will add punctuation to a story with no punctuation and practice reading it aloud with prosody. Focusing instruction on students' reading prosody can ultimately result in their increased comprehension of the text (Schwanenflugel et al., 2015).

Procedure

1. Choose a selection of narrative text with which students are familiar.

2. Remove all punctuation marks from the story and make copies for students to follow along with as you read the text aloud with no prosody.

3. Start a class discussion about how the punctuation marks in the story help students read with prosody and improved comprehension.

4. Project the first sentence of the reading selection so all students can see as you model how to add punctuation to this selected text.

5. Reread the text again, this time using obvious prosody.

6. Have students assist you as you add punctuation to the next sentence. Model reading this sentence aloud with prosody, then ask students to reread it using prosody. Check for students' understanding as they complete this task.

   Example:

   - *No punctuation*—The lightning flashed Dracula said The castle is cold tonight my dear I think we need a fire

   - *Punctuation added*—The lightning flashed! Dracula said, "The castle is cold tonight, my dear. I think we need a fire."

7. Ask students to work in pairs or small groups to add punctuation to the next two sentences, then have them take turns reading the sentences to each other with prosody.

8. As you complete this activity, direct students' attention to the way prosody can change and enhance the meaning of the text.

Evaluation

- Check for students' understanding of how punctuation influences prosody through their read alouds of the selected text.

Considerations

- A selection of narrative texts is recommended for this activity because this type of text is likely to include more instances of varying punctuation.
- Be sure students' prior knowledge includes identifying punctuation marks and their uses in text.

Noting Reading Punctuation   © wavebreakmedia/Shutterstock.com

Phrased Reading

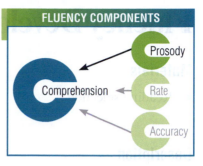

FLUENCY COMPONENTS

Prosody
Comprehension
Rate
Accuracy

Materials

- Reading selection; copies for each student
- Pencils for making slash marks

Use

- Whole Group
- Small Group
- Individual

Description

Phrased reading reinforces students' prosody when lumping text into syntactically coordinated units. This approach not only boosts students' reading fluency, but it helps them to construct meaning from the text, thus supporting their comprehension (Rasinski, Yildirim, & Nageldinger, 2011). In this phrased reading activity, you select a text and apply slash marks within the text to identify phrase boundaries you believe are appropriate. Then model how to read these phrases with prosody and provide opportunities for students to practice with your guidance. Finally, students will be provided a second reading selection where they will apply their knowledge of phrased reading to make their own slash marks and read the text with appropriate expression. Doing so will help build students' syntactic awareness and promote sensitivity to appropriate phrasing of text which can ultimately lead to increased comprehension (Rasinski et al., 2011).

Procedure

1. Choose a reading selection that students are familiar with that lends itself to expressive reading.
2. Using a pencil, apply slash marks to the text. Single slash marks should be used to indicate phrase boundaries. Double slash marks can be used in between sentences to indicate longer pauses.
3. Distribute copies of the text to students.
4. Read the text aloud to students using obvious expression within the phrased parts you mapped out. Discuss with students how your phrased reading allows for meaning making and how both your voice and pauses were used to indicate these phrases in your oral speech.
5. Employ Choral Reading (see page 49), and reread the selection with students, emphasizing the phrased units between the slash marks.
6. Provide an opportunity for students to reread the selection independently or in pairs while you provide immediate and explicit feedback.
7. Distribute a second reading selection for students without slash marks. Have students apply their knowledge of phrased reading to this selection by adding their own slash marks within phrased boundaries. Provide additional opportunities with additional selections if necessary.

Evaluation

- Meaningful phrase boundaries through the application of slash marks
- Words clustered into meaningful phrases as students read aloud
- Appropriate expression when their completed selections are read aloud with a partner or in front of a group

Considerations

- Teacher modeling of this activity is critical to students' attempts at successfully applying slash marks in appropriate syntactic units of the text.

Fluency Development Lesson

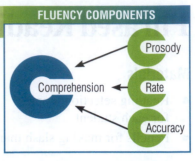

FLUENCY COMPONENTS

Materials
- Reading selection

Use
- Whole Group
- Partner

Description

The Fluency Development Lesson combines several oral reading strategies to create multiple opportunities for readers who struggle to hear and practice fluent reading (Padak & Rasinski, 2008). The lesson is designed to be used at least four times per week over an extended period of time, to encourage accurate word recognition and expression which ultimately contribute to thoughtful reading. This procedure involves reading to, with, and by students.

Procedure

1. Give students copies of a reading passage consisting of 50 to 200 words.
2. Read the text aloud while students follow along silently. This step may be repeated several times.
3. Discuss the content of the text with the students and encourage them to think about the way in which you read it aloud to them. Ask them how you used your voice, rate, and expression to help convey the meaning of the text.
4. Next, using Echo Reading (see page 48) and then Choral Reading (see page 49), have students read the text with you. It is important to continue to model fluent reading as students read with you and echo your reading.
5. When students appear to be developing proficiency and confidence in reading the text with you, have students form pairs.
6. Have student pairs move to various locations in the classroom. One student now reads the text aloud three times to their partner, while the partner follows along in the text. The listener provides help, if needed, and gives positive feedback such as, "You read all the words correctly," or "You really sounded excited when you read the part where they were running away from the bear."
7. Have students reverse roles so the reader becomes the listener and the listener becomes the reader. Repeat the above step.
8. Ask students to come back together as a whole group and ask for volunteers to read the text aloud to the entire group. At this time, the listeners do not follow along, but instead, enjoy the performance of their peers.
9. Praise students for their oral reading proficiency and their excellent listening behaviors.
10. Encourage students to take one copy of the passage home and read it to parents and relatives.
11. Put one copy of the passage into a notebook or folder for each student. Selected passages can be used for choral reading on successive days.

Evaluation

- Accuracy of word identification and self-correction behaviors
- Appropriate rate
- Appropriate expression

Assisted Reading

Providing Support for the Reader

Paired Reading

FLUENCY COMPONENTS

Materials

- Reading selection
- How Well Did Your Partner Read? reproducible for each student (page 64 or 65)

Use

- Partner

Description

Paired Reading, originally developed for use by parents and their children, is also a useful technique in the classroom (Topping, 1987a, 1987b, 1989, 2006). The tutor, a more capable reader, supports the tutee in reading materials that are generally more difficult than those read independently. In addition to supplying support in word recognition, the tutor also plays a major role in extending understanding of the text through discussion and questioning. Paired Reading has been found effective in improving accuracy and comprehension for students of all abilities between the ages of 6 and 13 (Topping, 1987a). The procedure for Paired Reading is easy to learn and implement in the classroom. Topping (1989) recommends that pairs work together three times per week for a minimum of six weeks, in sessions ranging from 15 to 30 minutes.

Procedure

1. Allow the tutee to select reading material within their instructional level.
2. Choose a comfortable place to read where both you and tutee can see the text easily. (See Tips When Reading with Your Partner on page 61.)
3. Begin by reading the text chorally (see page 49) at a speed that is comfortable for the tutee. If the tutee makes an error, say the word correctly. Have the tutee repeat the word and then proceed with choral reading. For example, if the tutee says "second" for "secret" in the sentence, "Gary promised to keep everything a secret," the tutor would stop reading and say "secret," the tutee would repeat the word "secret" and the pair would continue reading chorally.
4. If the tutee self-corrects a miscue, offer praise. Also praise the tutee if other self-monitoring behaviors are exhibited and for using good rate and prosody (stress, pitch, and phrasing).
5. If the text selected is at the tutee's independent reading level, the tutee can choose to read it aloud without the support of the tutor. When the tutee uses a prearranged signal (e.g., a tap or nudge), stop reading chorally with the tutee.
6. If the tutee encounters a difficult word, wait for five seconds. If the tutee does not correctly read the word, provide the word and return to reading chorally with the tutee.
7. Continue reading chorally until the tutee again signals that he or she wishes to read without support.
8. At the completion of the session, talk with the tutee about reading behaviors that are improving. (See Here Are Some Things You Might Say to Your Partner on page 61.) Note progress on the Paired Reading Record or Fluency Partners sheets (see pages 62–63) and/or on the sheets titled How Well Did Your Partner Read? (see pages 64–65).

Evaluation

- Quality of discussion about the selection
- Accuracy of word identification and self-correction behaviors
- Improvement in the items listed on the How Well Did Your Partner Read? reproducible

Tips When Reading with Your Partner

1. Sit closely enough together so that you can speak quietly to each other.
2. Sit so that you can both see the print.
3. Follow along when your partner is reading.
4. Encourage your partner.

Here Are Some Things You Might Say to Your Partner

1. You read that smoothly.
2. You read at a speed that sounded just right.
3. You read the words correctly.
4. You noticed the punctuation.
5. You remembered what you read.
6. You read with expression.
7. You are really improving!

Tutor _____ Tutee _____

Paired Reading Record

DATE	MATERIAL READ	BEHAVIORS NOTED	MINUTES OF READING (CIRCLE ONE)		
			5	10	15
			20	25	30
			5	10	15
			20	25	30
			5	10	15
			20	25	30
			5	10	15
			20	25	30
			5	10	15
			20	25	30
			5	10	15
			20	25	30

Name _____ Date _____

Title _____ Partner _____

Fluency Partners

Accuracy	**Speed**	**Expression**

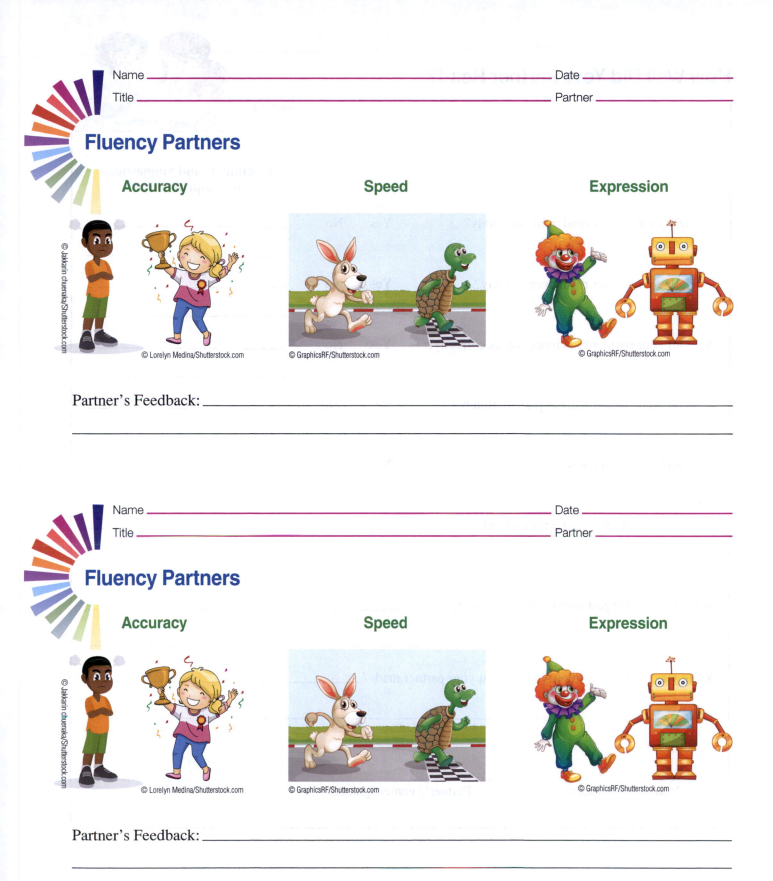

© Jakkarin chuenaka/Shutterstock.com

© Lorelyn Medina/Shutterstock.com

© GraphicsRF/Shutterstock.com

Partner's Feedback: _____

_____

Name _____ Date _____

Title _____ Partner _____

Fluency Partners

Accuracy	**Speed**	**Expression**

© Jakkarin chuenaka/Shutterstock.com

© Lorelyn Medina/Shutterstock.com

© GraphicsRF/Shutterstock.com

Partner's Feedback: _____

_____

How Well Did Your Partner Read?

© Thodoris Tibilis/Shutterstock.com

Comments and Suggestions for Improvement

1. Did your partner read more smoothly?   Yes   No   _____
                                                                _____

2. Did your partner read more quickly?   Yes   No   _____
                                                                _____

3. Did your partner read more words correctly? Yes   No   _____
                                                                _____

4. Did your partner use the punctuation better? Yes   No   _____
                                                                _____

5. Did it sound like it made sense?   Yes   No   _____
                                                                _____

6. Did your partner read with more expression? Yes   No   _____

What was the biggest area of need for your partner? _____

_____

What was the biggest improvement that your partner made? _____

_____

| _____ | _____ | _____ |
| Your name/signature | Partner's name/signature | Date |

How Well Did Your Partner Read?

Tutor _____ Tutee _____

What We Read _____ Date _____

Check (✓) what your partner did while reading.

__ Read Smoothly   __ Read Quickly

__ Knew Most Words   __ Used Punctuation Correctly

__ Used Good Expression   __ Sounded Like Talking

© Lorelyn Medina/Shutterstock.com

Tell your partner one thing that was better about his or her reading.

Have your partner circle the word or words that tells how well he or she thinks the reading went.

Terrible   Not So Good   OK   Good   Great

Choose one thing to work on next time you read together and write it below.

_____

Comments:

_____

_____

_____

_____

_____

_____

_____

_____

Neurological Impress

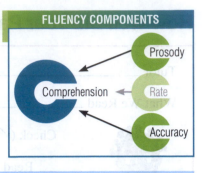

FLUENCY COMPONENTS

Prosody

Comprehension ← Rate

Accuracy

Materials

- Reading selection

Use

- Partner

Description

Neurological Impress involves the teacher and the student reading aloud simultaneously from the same book (Flood, Lapp, & Fisher, 2005; Heckelman, 1969). The teacher reads slightly faster than the student to keep the reading fluent. The teacher usually sits next to the student and focuses their voice near the ear of the student. The goal is to help students engage in a fluent reading experience. This method has demonstrated effectiveness in increasing reading fluency in students with disabilities (Ziadat & AL-Awan, 2018).

Procedure

1. Select an interesting book or passage that is appropriate for the student's reading level. It is recommended that you begin with reading materials that the student can read with at least 95% accuracy. You might want the student to choose materials from among several appropriate pre-selected items.

2. Relate the need to practice reading to some activity in which the student participates (e.g., soccer, swimming, or art). Stress that practice is necessary to excel in many activities, such as sports and reading. Tell the student that you will help the student practice by reading with him or her.

3. Have the student sit slightly in front of you so that your voice is close to the student's ear. Begin by reading the selected material out loud together. You should read a *little* louder and faster than the student.

4. Run your finger under the words simultaneously as the words are read. Have the student assume this task when he or she is confident enough. Make sure that print, finger, and voice operate together. You may want to assist the student by placing your hand over the student's and guiding it smoothly.

5. Reread the initial lines or paragraph several times together to build confidence and comfort with the method before proceeding to new material. As the passage is reread, drop your voice behind the student's, if you think he or she is gaining fluency.

6. Read for two to three minutes in the initial sessions. The goal should be to establish a fluent reading pattern. Appropriate intonation and expression in reading are vital. The major concern is with the style of the reading.

7. Supplement Neurological Impress with Echo Reading (see page 48) if the student has extreme difficulty with saying a word or phrase. Say the phrase and have the student repeat the phrase. When the student has satisfactorily repeated the phrase several times, return to the book or passage.

8. From time to time, speed up the pace for just a few minutes. Heckelman (1969) suggests using Neurological Impress daily for up to fifteen minutes to provide a total of ten hours of assistance. An alternative might be to use the method several times a week for several months. A paraprofessional or volunteer might be trained to work with individual students—especially students with disabilities and those who struggle with reading.

Evaluation

- Quality of phrasing and expression
- Increase in confidence while reading

Preview-Pause-Prompt-Praise

Materials

- Reading selection

Use

- Partner

Description

> Preview-Pause-Prompt-Praise is a peer tutoring technique used to develop self-monitoring and fluent reading (Allington, 2001; Corso, Funk, & Gaffney, 2001/2002). Pairs of students, often of differing ages or reading abilities, read together from the same text and support each other through the reading by using the Preview-Pause-Prompt-Praise technique. Allington (2001) recommends that parents, teachers, teaching assistants, and peers use a similar strategy when listening to students read aloud.

Procedure

1. Pair students with older or more able reading tutors.

2. The tutor *previews* the reading by discussing the cover and title of the book with the reader and then poses the question, "What do you think this will be about?" Several brief ideas may be shared with reasons offered. (See Tutor Guide on page 69.)

3. The tutee then begins reading aloud while the tutor listens, or the pair may read the first few sentences together chorally. If the reading is done chorally, the tutor discontinues reading along after the first few sentences, and the tutee continues to read aloud to the tutor.

4. If the tutee miscalls a word or appears to be having difficulty, the tutor should *pause* for three to five seconds to wait for the student to self-correct or read to the end of the sentence.

5. If the reader does not make a self-correction, decode the word, or reread the sentence correctly, the tutor provides *prompts* to assist the reader. For example:

   - If the word does not make sense, the tutor prompts with a clue to the meaning by saying, "Does that make sense? Does it sound right? What word would sound right?"

   - If the word makes sense, but it is incorrect, the tutor might prompt the tutee to look more carefully at the letters in the word by saying, "What does the word start with? Do you see a part of the word that you know? Can you reread, say the first sound, and see if the word falls out of your mouth?"

   - If the tutee stops, the tutor might say, "Go back to the beginning of the sentence and try reading it again."

   - If, after two prompts, the tutee still does not correct the problem, the tutor tells the tutee the word.

6. If the tutee self-corrects, or in some way fixes the problem, the tutor *praises* the tutee and invites him or her to continue reading.

7. After reading, the tutor *praises* something the tutee did well. For example, "I noticed that you stopped and went back when what you were reading didn't seem to make sense. That's something that good readers do."

8. The reading time concludes with the tutor asking, "What was your favorite part?" The tutor may also wish to share their favorite part as well.

Evaluation

- Quality of predictions
- Accuracy of word identification and self-correction behaviors
- Quality of sharing after reading

Peer Tutoring

© Tyler Olson/Shutterstock.com

Tutor _____ Name of Reader _____

Title of Selection _____ Date _____

Tutor Guide

1. TO BEGIN

Preview: Look at the cover and title of the book. Ask, **"What do you think this will be about?"**

"Let's start by reading together. When I stop reading along with you, you should keep reading."

2. DURING READING

Pause and Prompt: If the reader struggles and does not fix a problem, **pause** and slowly count to five. Then you might **prompt** by saying the following:

Does that make sense?

Does that look right?

Does that sound right?

What word would sound right? What does the word start with?

Do you see a part of the word that you know?

Go back to the beginning of the sentence and try reading it again.

3. AFTER READING

Praise: Tell the reader about something he or she did well. You might say, **"I noticed how you went back and figured out the word that you struggled with."**

Ask, **"What was your favorite part?"**

Then offer your favorite part. You might say, **"I really liked this part the best."** If your favorite part is the same one the reader chose, you might say, **"I liked that part, too!"**

Structured Repeated Reading

FLUENCY COMPONENTS

Comprehension → Prosody
Comprehension → Rate
Comprehension → Accuracy

Materials

- Reading selection
- Reading Progress Chart reproducible for each student (page 72)
- Stopwatch or watch with a second hand
- Calculator (recommended)

Use

- Individual

Description

Structured Repeated Reading is a highly motivating strategy that engages students in reading and rereading a text (Samuels, 1979). Structured Repeated Reading is considered "structured" because the miscues and words read per minute are recorded (see chart on page 71) to keep track of students' progress. Allington (2009) found that the rereading of texts as an intervention that develops fluency and accuracy is particularly effective for struggling readers. (The strategy is most effective when a more able reader models fluent reading followed by support through Choral Reading (see page 49) or other assisted reading techniques.) Using relatively easy texts and charting student progress also maximizes the positive effects of the strategy.

Procedure

1. Select a brief passage or story of 50 to 200 words for the student to read aloud. For beginning readers or readers who struggle, a passage of approximately 50 words is sufficient for the first time the strategy is used. The passage should be at an appropriate level of difficulty. That means that the student should generally recognize more than 90% of the words. If the passage contains 50 words, the student should generally recognize about 45 of the words. If the student misses more than 6 words in a 50-word passage, it is probably not suitable for use in repeated reading experiences.

2. Ask the student to read the passage orally. Using a copy of the passage, note the student's miscues and keep track of the time (in seconds) it took the student to read the passage.

3. Ask the student to tell you something about the passage or ask a question or two. Be sure that the student is not just calling words.

4. Record the time in seconds and the number of miscues as in the sample on page 71. In the example in the sidebar, the student read a 45-word passage in 58 seconds and made 4 miscues. To convert seconds into rate in words per minute (WPM), multiply the number of words in the passage by 60 and then divide by the time (in seconds) it took the student to read the passage. As noted in the example, the rate is approximately 46 words per minute (WPM).

$$\begin{array}{r} 46 \text{ WPM} \\ 58\overline{)2700} \\ \underline{232} \\ 380 \\ \underline{348} \end{array}$$

5. Encourage the student to practice rereading the passage independently for a day or two. The reading can be done both orally and silently. It can also be done at home. The goal is to have the student practice the passage several times before you next meet with the student to repeat the process described in Step 2.

6. Repeat the process of having the student read the passage to you. Record the time in seconds and the number of miscues on the chart under Reading 2. Continue this general procedure over a period of time, until a suitable rate is achieved. You can use your professional judgment to determine a suitable rate or refer to the norms or targets for oral-reading rates provided on pages 7 and 8. The chart on page 71 shows the five readings for a second-grade student over a 10-day period. The initial rate of 46 WPM was increased to approximately 87 WPM by the fifth reading. According to the norms provided for second graders in the spring of the year (see page 7), this student's rate is slightly below average.

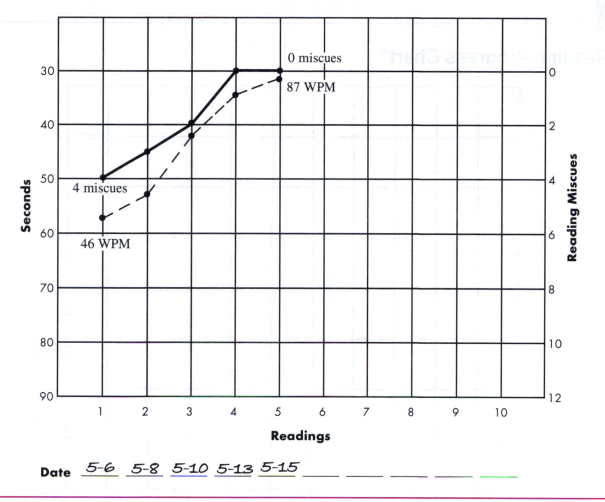

Seconds (left axis): 30, 40, 50, 60, 70, 80, 90

0 miscues

87 WPM

4 miscues

46 WPM

Reading Miscues (right axis): 0, 2, 4, 6, 8, 10, 12

Readings: 1 2 3 4 5 6 7 8 9 10

Date <u>5-6</u> <u>5-8</u> <u>5-10</u> <u>5-13</u> <u>5-15</u> ___ ___ ___ ___ ___

7. Repeat the strategy with a new selection. As you use the Reading Progress Chart on page 72, note that space is provided to record the date and to chart up to ten readings. You should base the actual number of readings on the student's progress in fluency. Some students will achieve a satisfactory level of fluency after a few readings; other students may need six or seven readings. Be flexible and responsive to individual differences. The Reading Progress Chart was designed to show visible evidence of gains. Students are encouraged as they see visible evidence of their progress and are motivated to improve their rate and accuracy. The charts can be a meaningful way to gather evidence of fluency development over time with a variety of passages. As a chart is completed for a passage, it can be placed in the student's work folder or portfolio.

Evaluation

- Decrease in miscues as noted on the Reading Progress Chart
- Increase in rate as noted on the Reading Progress Chart
- Appropriate expression

Student's Name _____ Title/Book _____

Reading Progress Chart*

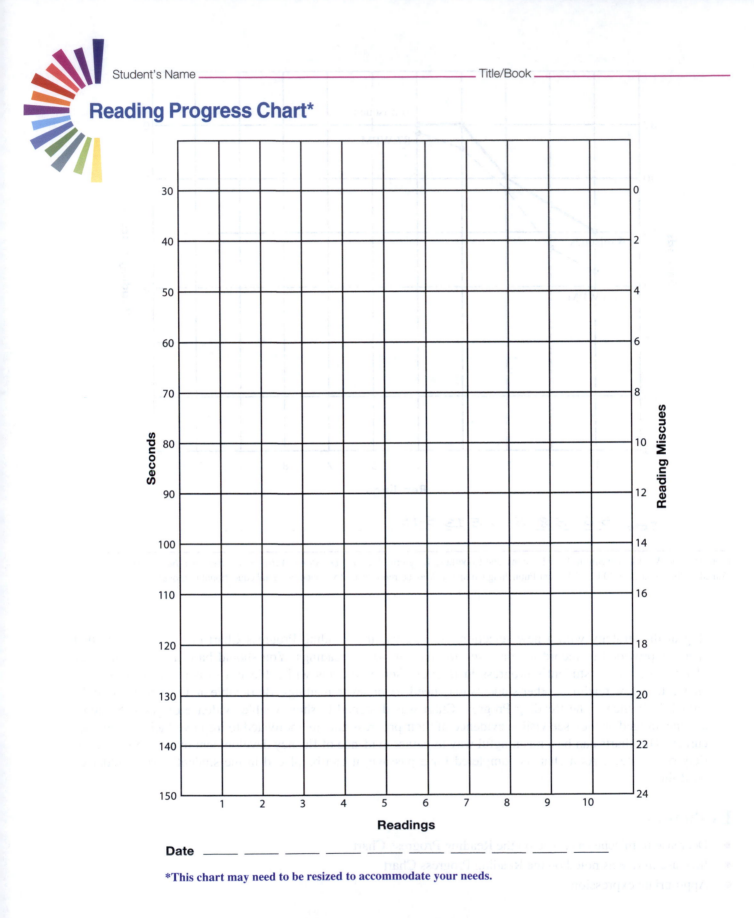

Seconds

	0
30	
40	2
50	4
60	6
70	8
80	10
90	12
100	14
110	16
120	18
130	20
140	22
150	24

Reading Miscues

1 2 3 4 5 6 7 8 9 10

Readings

Date _____ _____ _____ _____ _____ _____ _____ _____ _____ _____

*This chart may need to be resized to accommodate your needs.

Simplified Repeated Reading

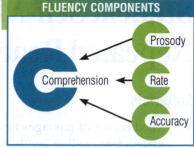

FLUENCY COMPONENTS

Materials

- Reading selection

Use

- Partner

Description

The method of Structured Repeated Reading (see page 70) was first introduced over 40 years ago (Samuels, 1979). More recently, Samuels (2002) simplified the method so that it does not require charting or computation of reading speed. In addition, after training, students can use it independently with minimal assistance from the teacher. Samuels recommends that Simplified Repeated Reading "should be used with students who are not yet automatic at word recognition, usually first and second graders" (Samuels, 2002, p. 178). This strategy is very similar to the Fluency Development Lesson (see page 58).

Procedure

1. Ask students how one becomes skilled in sports or some other activity with which students can relate. Guide the discussion as necessary so students realize that practice and repetition are key elements of becoming skilled. Then relate the process to reading.

2. Select appropriate materials for students to use. These materials can be from instructional materials or the classroom library.

3. Read the selected passage to the class while students follow along silently.

4. Assign each student to a partner. If possible, pair a proficient reader with a struggling reader. Once the reading begins, students will work on their own in pairs.

5. Have one student of the pair take the role of the teacher, and the other take the role of the student. Explain that the role of the student is to read the passage orally. The role of the teacher is to listen to oral reading while looking at the words in the text. This procedure allows both students to get practice with the passage. Model the process with a student if necessary.

6. Following the first reading, have students reverse roles and read. Switch roles two more times so that each passage is read four times.

7. Repeat the above process for each daily session. Samuels notes that "most of the gains in reading speed, word recognition error reduction, and expression in oral reading are acquired by the fourth reading" (Samuels, 2002, p. 178).

Evaluation

- Increase in accuracy in word identification
- Increase in rate
- Appropriate expression

Student Self-Managed Repeated Reading

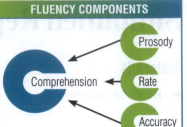

FLUENCY COMPONENTS

Comprehension — Prosody — Rate — Accuracy

Materials

- Typed copies of passages near students' independent reading levels, with word counts determined and noted
- Books or materials containing the original passages (optional)
- Stopwatches
- Calculators
- Pencils in various colors
- Folders and copies of the Untimed Repeated Reading Record sheet and the Timed Repeated Reading Record sheet reproducibles (pages 76–77)
- Student folders for completed Reading Record sheets
- Tape recorders and cassette tapes or digital voice recorder (optional)

Use

- Partner

Description

In this modified method of Repeated Reading (Samuels, 1979), student partners manage their own fluency development. Through modeling and scaffolding provided by the teacher, students are taught to note miscues and rate, calculate words correct per minute (WCPM), and complete record sheets of their progress (Moskal, 2005/2006). In addition to improving students' fluency, this approach can also increase students' self-efficacy and confidence, thereby motivating them to achieve reading success.

Procedure

1. Before students can successfully participate in the activity independently, it is necessary to engage them in several modeling and practice sessions lasting from 30–45 minutes each. Sessions include the components suggested by Johnson, Graham, and Harris (1997).

   - Show students the techniques required for conducting repeated readings of text—gathering necessary materials, reading passages orally, completing a mini-miscue analysis, calculating words correct per minute (WCPM), completing the Record Sheets, and putting materials away.

   - Begin by teaching students how to complete a mini-miscue analysis by misreading a passage of 20–30 words aloud to students, having them underline the miscues, and then discussing them. Note how miscues affect fluent reading.

   - Model how to track rate using a stopwatch and determine words correct per minute using a calculator.

   - Teach students how to complete each of the record sheets on pages 76–77.

   - During guided reading practice sessions, or in small group instruction, allow students to work in pairs to practice several of the Repeated Reading activities. Closely observe students and offer assistance as needed.

   - Students may need up to fifteen practice sessions before they can successfully complete all aspects of the Repeated Reading activity independently (Moskal, 2005/2006).

2. When you believe that students are ready to engage in the activity successfully, establish a designated area in your classroom for students to conduct Repeated Readings. Make sure that all necessary materials are readily accessible to students.

3. Select passages from materials that you have used in small group guided reading lessons and that are close to students' independent reading levels.

4. Assign student partners by selecting students who are "below or at the low end of the average words-correct-per minute rate range for their grade level or need assistance in prosody" (Moskal & Blachowicz, 2006, p. 79).

5. Have student pairs meet at the designated area. When both partners are ready, one student reads the typed copy or the material containing the original passage aloud while the listener carefully follows along with a copy of the same text. If the reader makes an error, the listener underlines the misread word using a colored pencil.

6. At the completion of the reading, the student listener asks the reader questions from the Untimed Repeated Reading Record sheet (see page 76).

7. The reader then completes the self-assessment section of the Untimed Repeated Reading Record sheet, records the number of miscues, and sets a fluency goal for the next reading of the passage.

8. Student pairs repeat the process, the listener recording miscues using a different colored pencil.

9. Following the second reading and recording, student partners switch roles. Then the entire process is repeated.

10. At the conclusion of the session, students file their completed record sheets in the designated folders.

11. Students can repeat the process up to five times using the same passage. During the final session, the listener can time the reading and record the words correct per minute (WCPM) on the Timed Repeated Reading Record sheet (page 77).

12. Students may also enjoy completing graphs of their progress showing changes in their rate and accuracy. (See Reading Fluency Charts on pages 78 and 79.)

Evaluation

- Increase in accuracy in word identification
- Increase in rate
- Appropriate expression
- Improvement in the items listed on the Untimed and Timed Repeated Reading Record sheets

Untimed Repeated Reading Record

Fluency Record

Name _____ Date _____

Title _____ Start Page _____ End Page _____

First Reading

How do you think you read? _____

How can your partner help you? _____

Did you understand what you read?   Yes   No   (If no, can your partner help?)

Number of Miscues _____

I used the punctuation correctly.	Almost Always	Sometimes	Rarely
I read with expression.	Almost Always	Sometimes	Rarely
I was able to read smoothly, without pausing a lot.	Almost Always	Sometimes	Rarely
The reading sounded like talking.	Almost Always	Sometimes	Rarely

Goal for next reading (circle one above)

Second Reading

How do you think you read? _____

How can your partner help you? _____

Did you understand what you read?   Yes   No   (If no, can your partner help?)

Number of Miscues _____

I used the punctuation correctly.	Almost Always	Sometimes	Rarely
I read with expression.	Almost Always	Sometimes	Rarely
I was able to read smoothly, without pausing a lot.	Almost Always	Sometimes	Rarely
The reading sounded like talking.	Almost Always	Sometimes	Rarely

I was able to reach my goal.   Yes   No

My goal for the next reading is _____

_____

_____

Adapted from Moskal, M. K. (2005/2006). Student self-selected repeated reading: Successful fluency development for disfluent readers. *Illinois Reading Council Journal, 34*(1), 3–11.

Timed Repeated Reading Record

Timed Reading Record

Name _____ Date _____

Title _____ Level _____

Start Page _____ End Page _____ Number of Words _____

First Reading

Number of Miscues _____   Number of Seconds _____

_____ words − _____ miscues = _____ ÷ _____ seconds × 60 = [   ] WCPM

I used the punctuation correctly.	Almost Always	Sometimes	Rarely
I read with expression.	Almost Always	Sometimes	Rarely
I was able to group words that went together.	Almost Always	Sometimes	Rarely
The reading sounded like talking.	Almost Always	Sometimes	Rarely

WCPM goal for the next reading [   ]

Second Reading

Number of Miscues _____   Number of Seconds _____

_____ words − _____ miscues = _____ ÷ _____ seconds × 60 = [   ] WCPM

I used the punctuation correctly.	Almost Always	Sometimes	Rarely
I read with expression.	Almost Always	Sometimes	Rarely
I was able to group words that went together.	Almost Always	Sometimes	Rarely
The reading sounded like talking.	Almost Always	Sometimes	Rarely

Did you reach your goal?   Yes   No   WCPM goal for the next reading [   ]

I still need to work on _____

_____

_____

_____

Adapted from Moskal, M. K. (2005/2006). Student self-selected repeated reading: Successful fluency development for disfluent readers. *Illinois Reading Council Journal, 34*(1), 3–11.

Reading Fluency Chart

Word Recognition Errors

Title _____   Title _____   Title _____

Number of Words Read _____   Number of Words Read _____   Number of Words Read _____

Word Recognition Errors	Readings			Readings			Readings		
	1	2	3	1	2	3	1	2	3
0									
1									
2									
3									
4									
5									
6									
7									
8									
9									
10									
11									
12									
13									

Name _____ Date _____

Reading Fluency Chart

Time in Seconds

Title _____   Title _____   Title _____

Number of Words Read _____   Number of Words Read _____   Number of Words Read _____

Time in Seconds	Readings			Readings			Readings		
	1	2	3	1	2	3	1	2	3
10									
15									
20									
25									
30									
35									
40									
45									
50									
55									
60									
65									
70									
75									
80									
85									
90									
95									
100									
110									

Whole-Class Repeated Reading

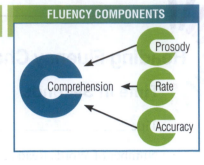

FLUENCY COMPONENTS

Materials

- Reading selection
- Anchor chart, DocCam with projector, or Smartboard

Use

- Whole Group

Description

This adaptation of repeated readings can be used with all groups of students; however, Monobe, Vintz, and McTeer (2017) recommend this for use with English Learners (ELs) as it helps them to "feel safe, develop confidence, and experience the joy of learning through meaningful social interaction with other students in the classroom" (p. 347). To effectively implement a whole-class repeated reading in your classroom, you should first review the thoughtfully chosen reading selection to identify any new vocabulary that students may need to have pre-taught. Translating these words would be especially helpful for ELs so they can better understand them in their first language. Whole-class repeated readings should be practiced daily for approximately 15 minutes using a pointer to follow along with the text as it is clearly displayed for the entire class to see.

Procedure

1. Carefully choose a reading selection, keeping in mind students' sociocultural needs. Monobe and colleagues (2017) recommend you consider the cultural implications of certain poems, songs, and children's literature that have embedded cultural meanings.
2. Display the reading selection for the entire class to see.
3. Model reading the selection aloud, using a pointer to follow along.
4. Have students read the selection aloud as a class while providing support with any new words.
5. Have students read the selection again on their own as a class.
6. Allow a student to lead the class in a final reading of the text selection using the pointer, taking on the teacher's role.

Evaluation

- Accuracy of word identification, appropriate rate, and expression similar to that modeled
- Observations of students' physical behaviors, affect or facial expressions, social interactions with other students, and their interaction with the text
- Students' engagement, motivation, and self-efficacy with language learning

Considerations

- You could extend this activity by providing students with a copy of the reading selection to take home to practice reading aloud with their families, thus bridging the gap between classroom learning and students' home lives.

Record, Check, Chart

Prosody

Comprehension

Rate

Accuracy

Materials

- Reading selection
- Copy of reading selection
- Digital voice recorder
- Three different colored pens, pencils, or markers
- Record, Check, Chart reproducible for each student (page 82)

Use

- Individual

Description

In this adaptation of repeated readings, students listen to recordings of their own reading and note their miscues. According to Allington (2001), the number of miscues generally decreases with each reading and fluency increases. In addition, having students note and chart their own progress is a visible record of their improvement and serves as an incentive to continue to work toward greater fluency.

Procedure

1. Have the student read aloud a text of appropriate difficulty and record it. An appropriate text for repeated readings is one that the student can read with at least 90% accuracy.
2. After making the recording, have the student listen and follow along in the text (or with a photocopy of the text).
3. As they listen to the recording, the student places a small check mark above each word that deviates from the text (e.g., omissions, insertions, mispronunciations).
4. Then have the student read and make another recording of the same passage. The student again notes, in a second color, any omissions, insertions, or mispronunciations with a check mark.
5. The student reads the same passage a third time, records the reading, listens again, and marks, in a third color, the deviations from text.
6. The student should tally and chart the number of text deviations for each reading, using the chart on page 82.
7. Meet with the student to discuss their progress. Give recognition for effort and progress.

Evaluation

- Reduction of miscues on the Record, Check, Chart reproducible
- Ability to monitor reading
- Accurate self-perceptions of improvement

Record, Check, Chart

Name _____ Date _____

Passage _____

RECORDING NUMBER	NUMBER OF CHECK MARKS (✓)	COMMENTS
1		
2		
3		

Name _____ Date _____

Passage _____

RECORDING NUMBER	NUMBER OF CHECK MARKS (✓)	COMMENTS
1		
2		
3		

Name _____ Date _____

Passage _____

RECORDING NUMBER	NUMBER OF CHECK MARKS (✓)	COMMENTS
1		
2		
3		

Reading While Listening

Materials

- Text selection for each student
- Text recordings of the reading
- Audio Books or Texts with CDs; Headphones
- Three different colored pens, pencils, or markers
- Reading While Listening Progress Chart reproducible for each student (page 85)

Use

- Small Group
- Partner
- Individual

Description

In Reading While Listening (or repeated listening), students listen to recorded passages while they silently read the written version (Kuhn & Stahl, 2000). Audio books are available commercially; however, in order to make the experience the most valuable, the recorded texts need to be at the students' instructional level and recorded at a speed that enables them to follow along. Cues need to be explicit (e.g., when to turn pages) to minimize students losing their places. Preparing recordings provides the optimal opportunity for students to gain from the experience. Students who become familiar with the procedure and are fairly fluent readers can also create their own recordings for classroom use (Rasinski & Padak, 1996). The advantage of Reading While Listening over Structured Repeated Reading (see page 70) or the Neurological Impress (see page 66) is that there is much less assistance needed from the teacher, because the modeling of fluent reading is provided by the recording. This makes the procedure more usable in a classroom setting where students are held accountable for reading the text fluently during Reading While Listening sessions, which is critical to the success of this activity.

Reading While Listening is also effective for students with learning disabilities, as well as for students who represent both the low-success and high-success range of readers in the classroom (Rasinski, 1990; Sindelar, Monda, & O'Shea, 1990). Kuhn and Stahl (2000) caution that it is important to make a distinction between Reading While Listening and classroom listening centers. Classroom listening center experiences generally do not include holding students responsible for reading the material in a fluent manner after repeated listening experiences; therefore, students do not practice reading the material, and may not make measurable gains in reading.

Procedure

1. Select materials that are of interest to students and that are challenging, but not at the students' frustration level.
2. Prepare recordings of the materials, using the following guidelines:
   - Read aloud at a comfortable rate, so that students can follow along.
   - Read with good phrasing and expression.
   - Give oral or auditory signal cues to students when a page should be turned.
   - If page layout makes it difficult for students to know where the reading will begin, tell them explicitly on the recording where to look when following along.
   - You may wish to encourage students to finger-point to the words as they listen or use an index card or paper marker to help them keep their places.

3. Provide several copies of the text so that a small group of students may participate in the activity simultaneously. See the list of suggested resources below.

4. Tell students that they are going to be listening to material that they will be expected to read aloud to you at a future date. Tell them that, after listening and following along several times, you will expect them to be able to read with expression, accuracy, and at a rate that sounds like they are talking.

5. Following the listening, have students practice reading the material several more times either independently and/or with a partner.

6. Finally, provide an opportunity for students to read the material aloud to you, an older student, a teaching assistant, or parent volunteer.

7. Track students' progress, paying particular attention to accuracy and rate (see Reading While Listening Progress Chart on page 85).

Evaluation

- Student engagement
- Improvement in items listed on the Reading While Listening Progress Chart

Suggested Resources

Kids.audible.com
This source provides digital audiobooks for download.

Green Eggs & Ham and other Servings of Dr. Seuss by Dr. Seuss.
This is an entire collection of Seuss' controlled vocabulary books.

Magic Tree House Books 1–4 by Mary Pope Osborne.
These are unabridged stories for listening and reading.

Owl Babies: Storybook Animations by Martin Waddell.
A DVD accompanies this book and has both a cued audio and an uncued audio.

We're Going on a Bear Hunt with CD by Michael Rosen.
Children enjoy listening to this favorite book as well as reading it themselves.

Name _____ Title of Selection _____ Level _____

Reading While Listening Progress Chart

FOCUS	1	2	3	4
Rate	Slow and laborious Struggles with words	Rate varies Some hesitations	Generally conversational Some smooth, some choppy	Conversational and consistent Smooth and fluent throughout
Prosody	Monotone	Monotone combined with some expression	Appropriate expression used much of the time	Appropriate expression maintained throughout
Phrasing	Word-by-word Long pauses between words	Some word-by-word, some phrases	Mostly phrases, some smooth, some choppy	Phrases consistently throughout, generally smooth and fluent
Punctuation	Little or no use	Uses some Ignores some	Uses most of the time	Uses consistently throughout

READING	DATE	TIME (IN SECONDS)	NUMBER OF MISCUES COUNTED AS ERRORS	HOLISTIC SCORE (CIRCLE A RATING IN EACH FOCUS AREA ABOVE AND ADD THE SCORES)
1				
2				
3				

Klassroom Karaoke

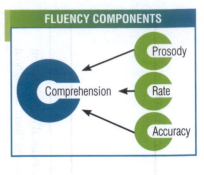

FLUENCY COMPONENTS

Materials

- Karaoke website
- Karaoke machine with CDGs
- Microphone (optional)

Use

- Whole Group

Description

Karaoke is the singing of songs using a recording without the lead vocals. Using karaoke helps students to build reading fluency through music. Children's songs, pop songs, and traditional folk songs are good choices for karaoke activities. Karaoke machines use compact discs with graphics (CDGs). Some online karaoke resources and CDGs are available in languages other than English. This feature makes them especially useful in bilingual classrooms.

Procedure

1. Set up the necessary equipment.
2. Begin with one of your favorite songs to teach the students.
3. Play the song while students follow along silently with the words on the screen.
4. Play the song again and pause the audio and video so students can read each screen aloud.
5. Play the song a third time and encourage the students to sing along with the vocals in unison.
6. In repeated experiences, students can then sing as a group, in trios, pairs, or solo.
7. If you choose to use the microphone, show students how it works.
8. Copy the text of the song for students to use in repeated readings. An adaptation might be to create the text in a cloze version, leaving out some of the vocabulary words, idioms, phrases, or English language structures. This adaptation is particularly useful for English Learners.
9. When students are comfortable with both the music and words, play the song without the vocal track and encourage students to sing along with the accompaniment.

Evaluation

- Accuracy of word identification
- Ability to follow along with words and music
- Appropriate expression

Suggested Resources

Karaoke for Kids! https://www.youtube.com/playlist?list=PL34A2C96C550F3AF0

Karafun https://www.karafun.com/karaoke/styles/kids/

RedKaraoke https://www.redkaraoke.com/

Thanks are extended to Ana Schmitz Viveros, a teacher of English Learners from Minneapolis, MN, for sharing this idea.

Performance Reading

Reading Aloud for the Enjoyment of Others

Say It Like the Character

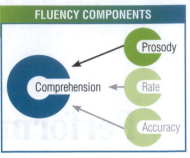

FLUENCY COMPONENTS

Materials

- Reading selection
- Sentence strips
- Emotion cards

Use

- Whole Group
- Small Group

Description

Say It Like the Character helps students learn to make inferences as they become more fluent readers (Opitz & Rasinski, 2008). When students read silently, they may not think about the way a character feels or how the character might speak. In Say It Like the Character, students are developing prosody as they are asked to read aloud using the intonation and expression they believe the character in the story might use when speaking. Thus, the story becomes more meaningful, and interpretations about the character are elicited.

Procedure

1. Ask students to read a given text silently. Be sure the selection contains character dialogue.

2. Select a segment of the text and ask students to reread it silently, thinking about how the character(s) might sound when speaking.

3. Invite a student or students to read the segment aloud in the way the character(s) might speak, thus conveying the feelings of the character(s) to the listener. You might use some of the following questions:

   - What emotion(s) were you conveying as you read to us?
   - What made you decide to read as you did?
   - Did you connect something in your own experience with that of the character(s)? If so, what?
   - Were there any typographic signals in the text that helped you know how to use your voice, for instance, large, bold type or exclamation marks?

4. As students continue reading silently, encourage them to pay attention to the events in the story, the typographical signals the author gives, and the ways the author helps the reader understand the character(s) and their feelings.

5. As a follow-up activity, you may wish to do the following:

   - Have students share the signals in the selection that they used to "say it like the character."
   - Select sentences from the text and print them on sentence strips. For example,

        "What is that crazy horse doing?" people asked one another.

        The ducks marched right out of the park in a straight line.

        Night came, and the lights went on in the city.

        "But wait! We need to get the camera."

        Waving his arms frantically, he shouted at the driver to stop.

        We worked side by side . . . long into the night.

        "Dress warmly, Jenny," her mom called.

        She swallowed hard, "I've learned a lot this summer."

- Print words that convey specific emotions on index cards. Some example words might be *fear, excitement, joy,* and *anger*.

- Invite students to choose one emotion card and one sentence strip and then read the sentence aloud, conveying the emotion on the card. Listeners might be invited to guess the emotion being expressed by the reader, thus turning it into a game and enhancing motivation for fluency practice (Person, 1993). (See Guess the Emotion on page 90.)

Evaluation

- Making appropriate inferences about character emotions
- Appropriate expression

Reading Aloud. Say it Like the Character

© LightFieldStudios/Shutterstock.com

Guess the Emotion

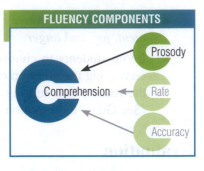

Materials

- Sentence strips
- Emotion cards

Use

- Small Group

Description

Guess the Emotion provides students with an opportunity to read brief sentences using their voices to convey a feeling. Their classmates, in turn, try to guess the emotion being expressed. This small-group activity is a pleasurable way for students to develop aspects of prosody: intonation, phrasing, voice quality, and attention to punctuation.

Procedure

1. Make a set of sentence strips for each small group of 5–7 students. Use the suggested sentences on page 91 or choose some from materials available in your school.

2. Prepare a set of emotion cards for each group (see pages 92–93). You may use the ones provided or create your own. You may wish to reproduce the emotion cards on card stock and laminate them for multiple uses.

3. Have students get into small groups. They can sit on the floor or around tables.

4. Place the sentence strips and emotion cards in two piles face down in the center of the group.

5. Begin by having one student draw a sentence strip from the pile. The student should first read the sentence silently and then orally for initial practice. If the student has difficulty with any of the words in the sentence, the student may ask for assistance from another member of the group.

6. Next, the same student draws an emotion card from the pile. The card is not shown to the rest of the group. The student rereads the sentence aloud using the expression or emotion indicated on the card. (If the expression/emotion card simply does not fit the sentence, the student may draw another card.)

7. Students in the group then guess which emotion the reader is conveying. You may wish to provide a list of emotions for students to consult.

8. When the emotion is guessed or told by the reader, the next student takes a turn until all in the group have had an opportunity to participate.

9. A variation of this activity is to provide the same sentence to all the students and have them draw different emotion cards. This variation conveys the ways the meaning of a sentence changes depending on the way it is read aloud.

Evaluation

- Communicating "emotional" meaning
- Appropriate intonation, phrasing, voice quality, and attention to punctuation

Thanks are extended to Susan Bolek, Maryanne Dihel, and Judy Martus, Community Consolidated School District 93, Carol Stream, IL for sharing this idea.

Sample Sentence Strips

1. The coach said, "I am a strong person, but she is stronger and smarter."

2. The lightning flashed! Dracula said, "The castle is cold tonight, my dear. I think we need a fire."

3. Bella said, "I am not afraid of the dark."

4. Dr. Frankenstein's monster said, "Don't be afraid. I won't hurt you."

5. The coach yelled, "Let's get back on defense!"

6. Snow White said, "I hope the seven dwarfs will be home soon. They are very late tonight."

7. The king said, "It is a cold day. Bring me my fur robe."

8. The mother said, "You are the nicest child in the whole world."

9. Superman said, "I must save the world from the evil Captain Crazy. He wants to destroy the city."

10. The teacher said, "Children, you must finish your homework tonight. There will be a test tomorrow."

11. Dad said, "Go upstairs and get your homework done right now."

Scared	Sweet
Excited	ANGRY
Happy	Sad
BORED	CONFUSED
SURPRISED	CONFIDENT

BRAVE	Silly
Nervous	**Threatening**

Just Joking

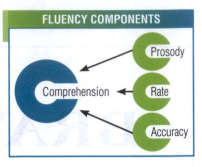

FLUENCY COMPONENTS

Prosody
Comprehension
Rate
Accuracy

Materials

- Selection of joke books
- Digital voice recorder (optional)

Use

- Whole Group
- Small Group
- Partner

Description

In Just Joking, students practice reading jokes for the purpose of developing prosody as well as for enjoyment of oral reading. Ness (2009) found that using jokes encouraged students to practice, rehearse, and re-read to improve their rate, expression, and use of punctuation leading to greater understanding of a joke's humor and to enhance enjoyment by an audience.

Procedure

1. Select materials at the student's instructional level.
2. Invite the student to read the joke silently, then orally to you. Take notes on the student's delivery, considering especially the student's accuracy, rate, and prosody. You may wish to use the rubric on page 133 for guidance. You also may wish to record this reading for use in later analysis by the student (see step 8).
3. Talk with the student about the joke, why it is funny, and how the delivery affects its understanding by an audience.
4. Call attention to any punctuation, stress, or other prosodic features that may affect the joke's meaning and humor. Remind the student why these features are used and how they give the reader signals for the delivery of the joke.
5. Following this brief discussion, read the joke aloud to the student. Invite the student to comment on your delivery and how it affected the joke's meaning.
6. Next, read one line or phrase of the joke to the student and ask the student to read it back just as you have read it (see Echo Reading on page 48).
7. Following Echo Reading, read the joke chorally with the student. Be sure to focus on intonation, timing, and emphasis on certain words to enhance the delivery of the joke for maximum humor.
8. Record the joke again and, if possible, have the student compare it to the recording of the first reading. Discuss the differences with the student and note why the second recording is more enjoyable and meaningful.
9. Put the student with a partner to read jokes that each have been practicing. You may wish to have students use the How Well Did Your Partner Read? reproducible on page 64 to help them give useful feedback to each other about their readings.
10. After adequate practice, designate a Just Joking day in your classroom where students present their jokes to their classmates. You may wish to duplicate the reproducible Laugh Meter (page 96) for your students to use in rating the jokes.

Evaluation

- Accuracy in pronouncing words
- Attention to punctuation
- Use of intonation and phrasing
- Enjoyment of reading and sharing reading with others

Suggested Resources

Connolly, S., & Barnham, K. (2012). *The monster fun joke book*. New York: Windmill.

Elliot, Rob. (2010). *Laugh-out-loud jokes for kids*. Grand Rapids, MI: Baker Publishing.

Horsfall, J. (2003). *Kids' silliest jokes*. New York: Sterling.

Keller, C. (2000). *Kids' funniest riddles*. New York: Sterling.

Kowitt, H. (2004). *This book is a joke*. New York: Scholastic.

McCarthy, R. (2008). *Waddle of laughs*. New York: Penguin.

Pattison, R.G. (2017). *Just joking LOL*. Washington, DC: National Geographic.

Rosenberg, P. (2011). *Sports jokes*. Mankato, MN: Child's World.

Weitzman, I. (2006). *Jokelopedia: The biggest, best, silliest, dumbest joke book ever*. New York: Workman.

Winn, W. (2016). *Lots of knock-knock jokes for kids*. Grand Rapids, MI: Zonderkidz.

Zonderkidz. (2015). *Lots of jokes for kids*. Grand Rapids, MI: Zonderkidz.

Helping a Student Practice Joke Delivery

© antoniodiaz/Shutterstock.com

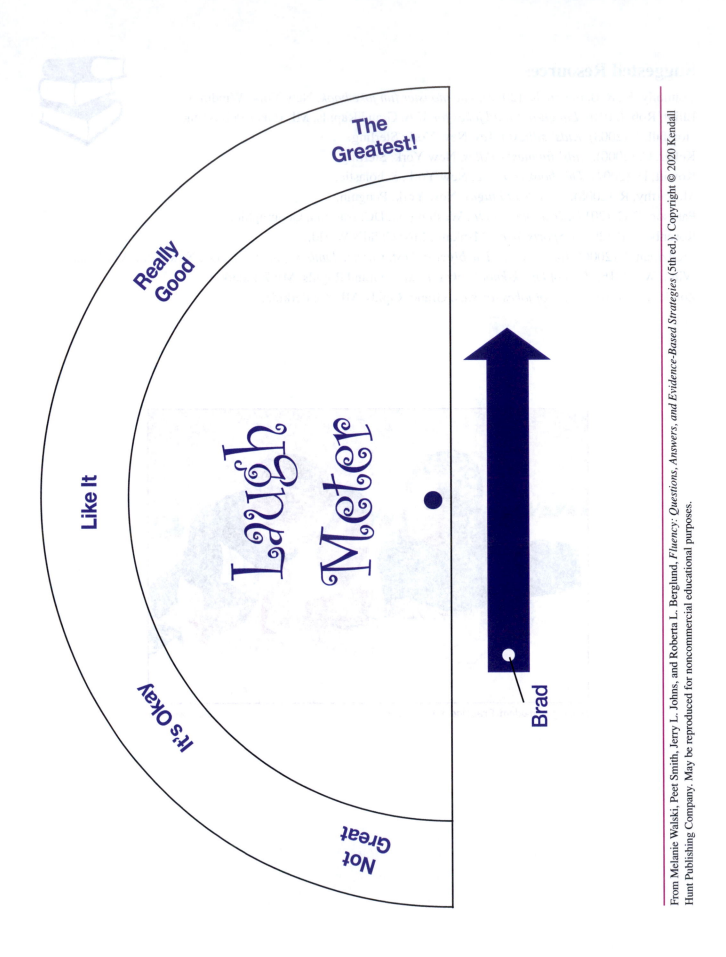

The Greatest!

Really Good

Like It

It's Okay

Not Great

Laugh Meter

Brad

Readers Theater

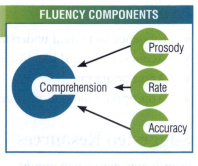

FLUENCY COMPONENTS

Prosody

Comprehension

Rate

Accuracy

Materials

- Readers Theater script for each student

Use

- Whole Group
- Small Group

Description

Readers Theater is a viable vehicle for oral reading fluency (Keehn, 2003) and a genuine way to promote repeated readings (Rasinski, 2000). It is a presentation of text read aloud expressively and dramatically by two or more readers (Young & Vardell, 1993). Meaning is conveyed to the audience, primarily through readers' expressive and interpretive readings rather than through actions, costumes, or props. Students can read from commercially prepared scripts or develop scripts from materials they are reading, either narrative or expository. General characteristics of Readers Theater include no full memorization of lines; holding scripts during the performance; no full costumes or staging; and narration providing a framework for the dramatic action conveyed by the readers. The primary aim of Readers Theater is to promote reading (Shepard, 1997), and it appears to do so, as the practice for a Readers Theater performance gives new purpose and added enjoyment for reading stories and books repeatedly. Martinez, Roser, and Strecker (1998/1999) offered an instructional plan for developing Readers Theater with young readers using narrative text, and Roser (2001) demonstrated that Readers Theater strategies can also help Hispanic middle-grade students learn to read in their second language of English. Flynn (2004/2005) suggested that having students write and perform scripts based on curriculum materials involves students in demonstrating comprehension, summarizing, synthesizing, and communicating information.

Procedure

1. Develop or select a script to be used with students. Such development may mean adding brief narration to describe the action in the story or dividing longer narrations into speaking parts for more than one narrator.

2. Read aloud from the story on which the script is based. Provide a good model of fluent reading.

3. Provide a brief lesson on one aspect of fluency, perhaps noting the signals in the text that might help students know how to read it aloud or discuss how the characters might be feeling at selected points in the story. This discussion should help provide insights about how each character might sound.

4. Distribute scripts to the students and have them read silently or with a buddy. You may want to encourage students to take the scripts home for additional practice.

5. The next day, have students practice reading the script aloud again; then determine who will be reading each role for performance purposes.

6. Have students spend the next day highlighting their parts in the script and reading and rereading their assigned roles with their group. Encourage students to think about how they might best convey the feelings of the character they are representing. They should also consider other ways they can help the audience understand the story and where they will stand or sit during the performance.

7. Finally, in front of an audience consisting of parents, school personnel, or other members of the class, have students perform their Readers Theater production. You may want to remind them to read like movie stars, not like robots!

8. Possible resources for Readers Theater scripts are listed on the next page.

Evaluation

- Evidence of textual understanding through the use of appropriate gestures, facial expressions, and voice
- Accuracy of word identification
- Appropriate rate
- Appropriate intonation, phrasing, voice quality, and attention to punctuation

Suggested Resources

http://www.aaronshep.com/rt

http://www.readingrockets.org/strategies/readers_theater

http://www.readwritethink.org/professional-development/strategy-guides/readers-theatre-a-30703.html

https://www.scholastic.com/librarians/programs/whatisrt.htm

https://www.waikoloaschool.org/apps/video/watch.jsp?v=144043

Braun, W., & Braun, C. (2000). *A readers' theatre treasury of stories.* Calgary: Braun & Braun.

Dixon, N., Davies, A., & Politano, C. (1996). *Learning with readers theatre.* Winnipeg, MB: Peguis.

Fredericks, A. (2000). *Silly salamanders and other slightly stupid stuff for readers theatre.* Portsmouth, NH: Teacher Ideas Press.

Glasscock, S. (2000). *10 American history plays for the classroom.* New York: Scholastic.

Ratliff, G. L. (1999). *Introduction to readers theatre: A classroom guide to performance.* Colorado Springs, CO: Meriwether Publishing.

Shepard, A. (2004). *Folktales on stage: Children's plays for reader's theater.* Redondo Beach, CA: Shepard.

Sloyer, S. (2003). *From the page to the stage: The educator's complete guide to readers theatre.* Westport, CT: Teacher Ideas Press.

Walker, L. (1997). *Readers theatre strategies for the middle and junior high classroom.* Colorado Springs, CO: Meriwether Publishing.

Wallace, N. K. (2016). *Ghosts and gummy worms: A readers' theatre script and guide.* Minneapolis, MN: Magic Wagon.

Wallace, N. K. (2016). *Turkey and takeout: A readers' theatre script and guide.* Minneapolis, MN: Magic Wagon.

Wallace, N. K. (2016). *Medals and memorials: A readers' theatre script and guide.* Minneapolis, MN: Magic Wagon.

Performance Poetry

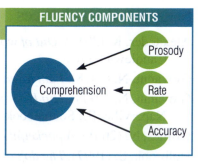

FLUENCY COMPONENTS

Materials

- Poetry selections

Use

- Partner
- Individual

Description

Repeated Reading, a procedure where students read a selected passage several times over a period of days, has been found to be an effective strategy to help improve students' fluency (Rasinski, Padak, Linek, & Sturtevant, 1994). In Performance Poetry (Faver, 2008/2009), students read poems over the course of several days and perform them for their classmates. Because poetry is a genre that students especially enjoy, they are motivated to practice their poems and are excited about sharing them with their peers. Stanley (2004) suggests that reading and performing poetry offers multiple opportunities for students to pleasurably develop fluency as well as the essential areas of phonemic awareness, vocabulary, phonics, and comprehension.

Procedure

1. Read several poems and select those containing rich and/or playful language that are appropriate for the ages of your students.

2. Read the selected poem to your students, modeling effective oral reading behaviors. Discuss with students the various aspects of fluency: rate, accuracy, and prosody.

3. Discuss the poem, focusing on any difficult words as well as the rhyme, rhythm, and punctuation.

4. Read the poem chorally with the whole group. Discuss any difficulties students appear to have. Focus on the enjoyment of the language in the poem and any visual images that the words create.

5. Place each student with a partner. You may want to consider pairing a more able student with a less able student. Also, consider pairing those students who will be able to work well together.

6. Invite students to continue to practice the poem for 5–10 minutes, first chorally, then taking turns reading it aloud to their partners.

7. Continue the choral reading and partner reading for several days until students appear to be fluent and comfortable reading the piece.

8. At the conclusion of each daily practice session, invite those students who feel ready to read the poem aloud to the rest of the group to do so.

9. Invite those listening to give the reader feedback on fluency, which elements were especially good, and those that might need more practice.

10. Periodically, you may want to have students select their favorite poems to share with a wider audience. Faver (2008/2009) suggests using your school's morning news or having your class take a poetry tour to other classrooms for poetry sharing.

Evaluation

- Acceptable rate
- Appropriate phrasing
- Improved expression

Suggested Resources

Alexander, K. (2017). *Out of wonder: Poems celebrating poets*. Somerville, MA: Candlewick Press.

Giovanni, N. (2018). *I am loved*. New York: HarperCollins.

Giovanni, N. (2008). *Hip Hop speaks to children: A celebration of poetry with a beat*. Naperville, IL: Sourcebooks, Inc.

Grimes, N. (2001). *A pocketful of poems*. New York: Clarion Books.

Holbrook, S. (1997). *The dog ate my homework: Poems*. Honesdale, PA: Boyds Mills Press.

Katz, A. (2009). *Going, going gone! And other silly dilly sports songs*. New York: Simon & Schuster.

Lansky, B. (2001). *My dog ate my homework: A collection of funny poems*. Minnetonka, MN: Meadowbrook Press.

Lansky, B. (2000). *If pigs could fly*. Minnetonka, MN: Meadowbrook Press.

Prelutsky, J. (1990). *Something big has been here*. New York: Greenwillow Books.

Silverstein, S. (1974). *Where the sidewalk ends*. New York: HarperCollins.

Students Enjoying a Poetry Performance

© Africa Studio/Shutterstock.com

Independent Reading

Reading on Their Own

Read and Relax

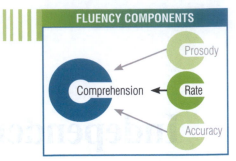

FLUENCY COMPONENTS

Prosody · Comprehension · Rate · Accuracy

Materials

- Reading selections
- Rules for Read and Relax reproducible for each student (page 104) (optional)

Use

- Whole Group
- Individual

Description

Read and Relax is an adaptation of Sustained Silent Reading (SSR) (see page 105) developed for use in primary grade classrooms (Maro, 2001, 2004). Similar to Sustained Silent Reading, all students read silently for a given amount of time each day. One major difference between Sustained Silent Reading and Read and Relax is that Read and Relax requires students to read materials that are at their independent reading levels—text that can be read with 99% accuracy in word recognition and 90% comprehension (Johns, Elish-Piper, & Johns, 2017). Another difference is that the teacher uses think-alouds to help students understand how to select materials and use metacognitive comprehension strategies when reading independently. Also, in Read and Relax, the teacher monitors students' reading by asking students to read portions of the text aloud to the teacher. The opportunity for students to self-select materials and read them for an uninterrupted period of time increases the number of words read and also increases students' involvement in the reading process. Through the process of reading many easy books, students become more fluent readers and gain competence and confidence (Gillet, Temple, Temple, & Crawford, 2016).

Procedure

1. A well-supplied classroom library that contains materials at a wide variety of levels and interests is essential to Read and Relax.

2. Gather a few books from the classroom library and model a Read and Relax session for your students. Gather students around you and explain that you are going to show them what Read and Relax looks like so that they will know what to do when it is their turn to Read and Relax. Explain to students that they will read their selections silently.

3. Open your first book and make a prediction about its content. Begin to read aloud and reflect on your predictions, making your thinking apparent to your students. Continue to read aloud, sharing your reading and your thinking as you read. You may want to show students how you ask questions and make connections as you read. For example, when reading a book about cats, you might say, "My cat falls asleep after she eats, just like the cat in this story. I wonder if cats need a special place to sleep or if they just fall asleep anywhere. Maybe I will find out as I continue to read this book."

4. In order to demonstrate what to do when a book is too difficult, struggle with some words in one of your Read and Relax books. After struggling with several words, tell your students that you can't relax with this book; therefore, it is too difficult for your Read and Relax time. Put it down and begin to read another book, modeling fluent reading. Explain that with an easy book, you can say almost all the words and understand the story. Tell students that they should read easy books during their Read and Relax time, books that they can read comfortably.

5. On another day, invite students to select books and get ready for Read and Relax time. Remind them of the rules for Read and Relax, such as no talking to other students and always having several books ready to read. You may wish to post the rules so students can refer to them as needed.

6. Once Read and Relax has begun and students appear to be able to follow the behavioral guidelines, you may then begin to monitor students as they are reading. Quietly stop by students' desks and ask individual students to read some of their books to you. If the student is struggling when reading and doesn't sound relaxed, encourage the student to find an easier, more suitable, text. You might say, "You are working too hard. Find a book that you will feel more relaxed reading."

Evaluation

- Rate indicating that the materials are "just right" for the student
- Appropriate text-related comments and questions
- Increased confidence in reading selected materials
- Improvement in items listed on the Rules for Read and Relax reproducible

Reading Silently during Read and Relax   © Rawpixel.com/Shutterstock.com

- Find books that are easy for you to read by yourself, books that you can read comfortably.

- Have your books ready for Read and Relax time.

- If you need to, get a drink and go to the bathroom before Read and Relax begins.

- Keep your hands and feet to yourself.

- Keep reading. Stop only when your teacher tells you to.

Sustained Silent Reading (SSR)

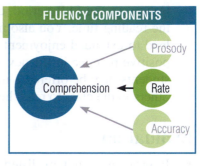

FLUENCY COMPONENTS

Materials

- Reading selections
- Sharing Your Reading reproducible for each student (page 107)
- Rules for SSR Time reproducible for each student (page 108) (optional)

Use

- Whole Group
- Individual

Description

Sustained Silent Reading (SSR) encourages students to practice reading self-selected materials, during a designated time in the school day (Berglund & Johns, 1983; Pilgreen, 2000; Krashen, 2004). The purpose is to provide an opportunity for students to develop fluency and, at the same time, expand their vocabulary and comprehension abilities (Gillet, Temple, & Crawford, 2004). It is especially vital to tap into students' intrinsic motivations to read during SSR not only so they stay on task, but because of the effect it has on their reading comprehension. That is, when students are intrinsically motivated to participate in silent reading their reading comprehension increases (Guthrie & Cox, 2001; Guthrie, Hoa, Wigfield, Tonks, & Perencevich, 2006). Sustained Silent Reading provides an opportunity for all students to build fluency in their reading through regular opportunities to practice (Pearson & Fielding, 1991). Successful reading practice develops rapid, flexible word identification skills and strategies, builds vocabulary, and contributes to overall reading comprehension.

Procedure

1. Tell students that they will be having an opportunity to choose something that they would like to read and to read it for a specified period of time. Provide an opportunity for students to locate the materials and have them ready for the SSR period.

2. Designate a specific time during the day when all students will participate in SSR. Some teachers choose to do this during reading workshop or during self-selected reading time, if they are using the four-block model (Cunningham, 1999).

3. Go over the procedures and guidelines so that students understand expectations during SSR. See page 108 for some suggested Rules for SSR Time, adapted from Anderson (2000). A useful handbook for organizing and managing an SSR program has been prepared by Pilgreen (2000).

4. Start with a short period of time, especially for young or less able students. Expand the time as students appear ready. When students ask if they can continue reading after the time is up, consider that a signal to increase your SSR time.

5. Provide materials for students who can't find something to read or who run short of materials before the time is up.

6. Be a model of good reading yourself. Students will be interested in what you are reading and will grow to understand that adults, as well as students, choose to read for pleasure, both in and out of school. (Some teachers choose to balance modeling reading with conferring with their students about their reading. At least two days a week they read during SSR and on the other days, they confer with their students.)

7. Following the SSR period, compliment students on their behavior and their consideration of others during the reading time. You also may invite students to comment on their reading, if they wish. Comments may lead to extended enjoyment and to spontaneous sharing of text segments, thus promoting meaningful and positive practice in fluency and creating desire in others to read the same materials at another time. A few students may be offered a more extensive opportunity to tell about their reading (3 minutes) and persuade others in the class to read the same materials. (See the Sharing Your Reading chart on the following page.)

Evaluation

- Improvement in items listed on the Sharing Your Reading reproducible
- Improvement in items listed on the Rules for SSR Time reproducible
- Rate indicating that the materials are of an appropriate level of difficulty for the student
- Increased confidence in reading selected materials

Engaging in Sustained Silent Reading   © Anna Chelnokova/Shutterstock.com

Sharing Your Reading

- You have a maximum of three minutes to tell the group about your reading today.

- If you read fiction, you must include:

  - title
  - author
  - where it took place (setting)
  - the main character(s)
  - one part that you liked best

- If you read for information, you must include:

  - title
  - author
  - what the reading was mostly about
  - one thing that you learned or found interesting from your reading

- Tell us if you would recommend the reading to others and why or why not.

- Choose three of your classmates to ask you questions about your reading or to comment on your sharing.

Rules for SSR Time

- Choose more to read than you think you will need.

- Have your materials ready before SSR time begins.

- If needed, get a drink and take a restroom break before SSR time begins.

- Find a comfortable place to read and stay there during SSR time.

- Keep your hands and feet to yourself. Stretch your arms out and be sure you cannot touch anyone else from where you are sitting in your reading place. If you can touch someone, move before you begin to read.

- Keep reading. Don't notice anything else while you are reading. The only exceptions are a fire drill, disaster drill, a call to the office, or instructions from your teacher.

- Stay quiet. Noise of any kind disturbs others and prevents you and them from reading.

Fluency Jars

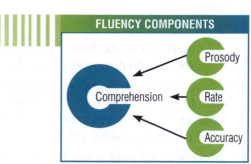

FLUENCY COMPONENTS

Prosody

Comprehension

Rate

Accuracy

Materials

- Jars, materials to decorate and personalize
- Cards to fill the jars; fluency phrases or sentences, basic sight vocabulary cards (see pages 34–38), emotion cards (see pages 92–93)

Use

- Individual

Description

Students can practice their fluency skills independently using Fluency Jars. You can incorporate these jars as part of a literacy center in your classroom, or students can have their Fluency Jars on-hand when they complete a task early or just need additional practice during a fluency lesson. Each jar is filled with materials that is on a student's independent level, so selections for these materials should be made by the teacher and with students' input. Give students options for each card/strip they pull from the jar. For instance, if a student pulls an emotion card from the jar, have them read a book, poem, etc. using that emotion. If a student pulls a basic sight vocabulary card, have them write a sentence with the selected vocabulary word, and then read their sentence aloud. The possibilities for each card/strip are limitless!

Procedure

1. Have students personalize their Fluency Jars by decorating and putting their names on them.

2. Next, fill the Fluency Jars with various fluency materials such as phrase cards, sentence strips, basic sight vocabulary cards, and emotion cards. You might want to fill the jar with one type of material (e.g., all phrase cards or all sentence strips), so students always know what to do when they pull a card from the jar. Then change the contents of the jars periodically so students have access to various types of materials.

3. Model how to pull a card from the jar and practice reading it independently.

4. Allow students to pull a card from the jar and practice their fluency skills with each selection. Provide guidance for students as they practice each type of card to ensure successful completion of this activity when they practice independently later.

5. Provide opportunities for students to practice independently with the materials in their fluency jars.

Evaluation

- Check that students understand the expectations for each type of card pulled from their Fluency Jar.
- Evaluate students on how effectively they demonstrate their understanding of each card/strip that they pull from the jar. This will vary based on the type of card they pull.

Considerations

- The materials in the Fluency Jars should be updated often so that students have new challenges and have opportunities to demonstrate a wide variety of fluency skills.

- Make sure students understand the expectations for each type of card they pull from the Fluency Jars. You can do this by modeling the various Fluency Jar activities for each type of card pulled or providing an anchor chart or direction sheet with directions on what to do with each type of card they pull from the jar. (See example on page 111.)

- Modeling and guided practice is essential for students' success with this activity.

- Be sure to use durable jars that are suitable for extended use.

Directions for Fluency Jar Cards

IF YOU CHOOSE . . .

AN EMOTION CARD	A SIGHT WORD	A POETRY STRIP	A PUNCTUATION SENTENCE	A FLUENCY PHRASE
Choose a book from the classroom library that you've read before and read the book using the emotion on your emotion card.	Practice saying the sight word **FIVE** times. Write your sight word in a sentence. Read your sentence **FIVE** times.	Read the poem quietly to yourself.	This card doesn't have any punctuation marks. Read it aloud **TWO** times without using any expression. Write in the punctuation marks on your card. Read it **TWO** more times using expression.	Read your fluency phrase **FIVE** times.

Fluency Walkabout

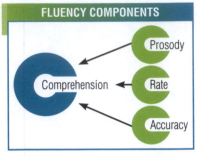

FLUENCY COMPONENTS

Materials

- Fluency resources hung up and stored around the classroom (e.g., pocket charts with fluency phrases or sentences, basic sight vocabulary cards; anchor charts with previous fluency lessons; Readers Theater scripts (see page 97); poetry strips; song lyrics from Klassroom Karaoke (see page 86).

Use

- Individual

Description

Fluency Walkabouts get students up out of their seats and moving around the classroom. Movement in the classroom has been shown to improve on-task behavior (Mahar, Murphy, Rowe, Golden, Shields, & Raedeke, 2006) and increase students' perceived competence and effort in academic tasks (Vazou, Gavrilou, Mamalaki, Papanastasiou, & Sioumala, 2012). It also reinforces the concept that students need fluency to successfully navigate the spaces around them (e.g., classrooms, schools, communities), and not just a skill needed to read and comprehend books. This activity would be best suited for use during literacy centers in which students are familiar with established routines, including walking around the classroom independently to read various print materials.

Procedure

1. Hang up various fluency materials in easily accessible locations around the classroom. These materials should include texts that students are familiar with, so be sure to save fluency phrases, sentences, basic sight vocabulary cards, and poetry strips to place in pocket charts. You may also want to display anchor charts from previous fluency lessons, scripts from previous Readers Theater lessons and song lyrics from Klassroom Karaoke activities.

2. Model how to (a) navigate the classroom space to access the fluency materials placed around the room, (b) select fluency materials, and (c) practice reading these materials independently and quietly.

3. Allow students to walk freely around the classroom to locate the fluency materials and practice reading them independently. Provide support to students as they first practice these routines.

4. During literacy centers, encourage students to practice the routines of the Fluency Walkabout while they also practice their fluency skills independently.

Evaluation

- Increased confidence reading selected materials
- Navigation of classroom space and activity routines

Considerations

- Be sure to keep materials at students' eye-level so they can access them easily and independently.
- A similar anchor chart or direction sheet as the one used in the Fluency Jars activity (see page 111) with directions on what to do with each type of fluency material may be useful here. An example of one type of activity you could use for a Fluency Walkabout is included on the next page.

Fluency Walkabout Activity

Read over this list of high-frequency nouns to yourself. Give yourself a pat on the back each time you say a word correctly and without pausing. When you run into a word that gives you trouble, use a notecard to write it down so you can practice it throughout the day.

air	group	people
back	hand	place
book	head	road
boy	home	room
car	house	school
children	man	side
city	men	table
day	money	thing
dog	morning	time
door	mother	top
eye	Mr.	town
face	Mrs.	tree
father	name	water
feet	night	way
friend	nothing	year
girl		

Integrated Strategies

Developing Fluent Readers Incorporating Writing, Speaking, and Listening

Oral Recitation Lesson

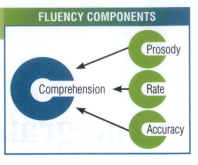

FLUENCY COMPONENTS

Materials

- Reading selection for each student
- Story Map reproducible for each student (pages 118–119)

Use

- Whole Group
- Small Group
- Partner

Description

Research shows that some form of oral reading fluency instruction is needed for developing readers. However, considerations need to be made for the individual needs of students, the instructional context, and instructional approach of the teacher (Rasinski & Hoffman, 2003). The Oral Recitation Lesson is a structured process that involves both direct and indirect instruction using narrative text. The lesson includes the modeling of effective oral reading and both guided and independent practice. Reutzel and Hollingsworth (1993) and Reutzel, Hollingsworth, and Eldredge (1994) found that the Oral Recitation Lesson improves both fluency and reading comprehension.

Procedure

1. Read a story aloud to students.

2. Following the reading, elicit the major story elements, including setting, characters, major events, and solution. Individually or as a group, complete a story map graphic organizer. See pages 118 and 119 for examples of reproducible story maps.

3. Using the story map as a guide, help students write a summary of the story. For students with little experience in summary writing, model how to write a summary using the information from the story map. For students who are more familiar with summary writing, you might use shared or interactive writing to complete the story summary. More advanced or more able students may be able to complete the summary independently.

4. Following the completion of the story map and summary, read aloud a selected portion of the story, perhaps one that was particularly exciting, meaningful, or eventful.

5. After reading the segment of the text aloud, have students read it chorally (see page 49) with you until they appear to be reading with good rate, accuracy, and expression.

6. Next, put students into pairs and have them read the story segment to each other. Ask students to read the passage just as you have practiced it together. Remind students that effective oral reading involves reading like they are talking, with accuracy and expression, for the purpose of communicating understanding.

7. When students have completed the partner reading, read aloud another portion of the text and follow it with Choral Reading (see page 49) and partner reading, until several segments of the text have been modeled and practiced.

8. On another day, ask students to select one of the modeled and practiced passages and read it aloud to a peer group. Following each reading, ask listeners to make one or two positive comments about each reader's performance.

9. On successive days (usually two to four), ask students to read aloud in a soft voice to themselves for about ten minutes, using the same passages previously practiced. Move around the class or group and listen to students as they read, providing feedback as appropriate.

Evaluation

- Quality of completed Story Map
- Active involvement in the group and partner readings
- Quality of soft voice reading (accuracy, rate, and prosody) as you move about the room

Sharing Story Segments

© Monkey Business Images/Shutterstock.com

Story Map

Title

Setting

Characters

Problem

Events

Solution/Outcome

Based on Beck and McKeown (1981).

From Melanie Walski, Peet Smith, Jerry L. Johns, and Roberta L. Berglund, *Fluency: Questions, Answers, and Evidence-Based Strategies* (5th ed.). Copyright © 2020 Kendall Hunt Publishing Company. May be reproduced for noncommercial educational purposes.

Name _____

Date _____

Story Map

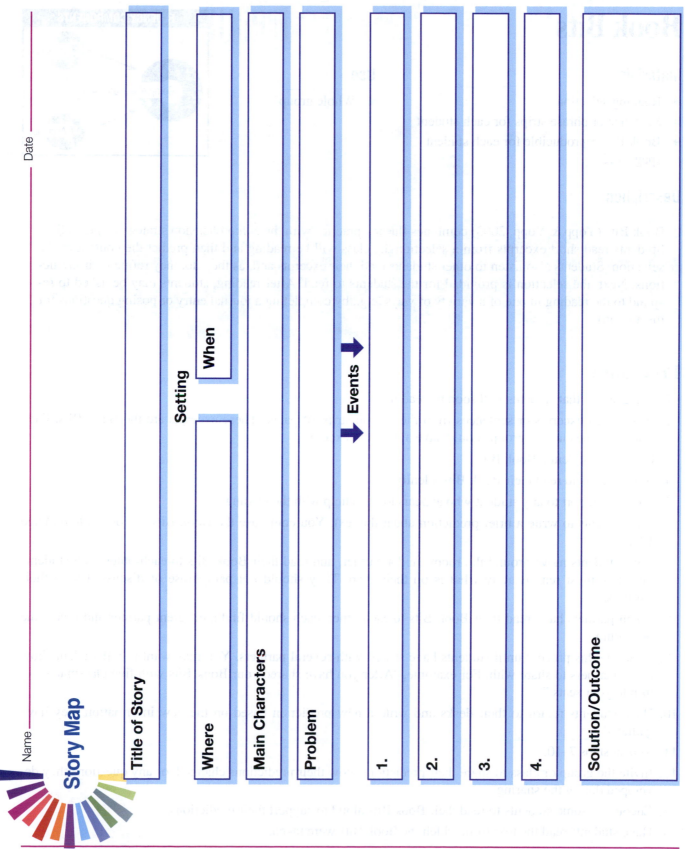

Title of Story

Setting
- Where
- When

Main Characters

Problem

Events →

1.

2.

3.

4.

Solution/Outcome

Based on Beck and McKeown (1981).

From Melanie Walski, Peet Smith, Jerry L. Johns, and Roberta L. Berglund, *Fluency: Questions, Answers, and Evidence-Based Strategies* (5th ed.). Copyright © 2020 Kendall Hunt Publishing Company. May be reproduced for noncommercial educational purposes.

Book Bits

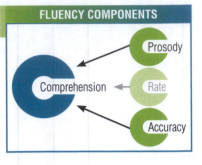

FLUENCY COMPONENTS

Prosody
Comprehension ← Rate
Accuracy

Materials

- Reading selection
- Sentence or phrase strips for each student
- Book Bits reproducible for each student (page 122)

Use

- Whole group

Description

Book Bits (Yopp & Yopp, 2003) combines fluency practice with the comprehension strategy of prediction. Students read short excerpts from a selection the class will be reading and then predict the content of the selection. Students also listen to other students read their excerpts and, as they do, they refine their predictions. Next, the selection is provided for the students to read. After reading, students may be asked to respond to the reading in one of a variety of ways (e.g., by completing a journal entry or posing questions for discussion).

Procedure

1. Select a text that students will soon be reading.
2. Write short excerpts or sentences from the text on strips of paper. These excerpts are the Book Bits. Each student in the class or group should have a different excerpt.
3. Give each student a Book Bit.
4. Ask students to read their Book Bits silently.
5. Provide support to any student who appears to need help with the reading.
6. Ask students to write a brief prediction about the text. You could use the Book Bits reproducible on page 122.
7. Have students move around the room, find a partner, and read their Book Bits to each other. Tell students that they must read exactly what is on their strip. They should not paraphrase or discuss it with their partners.
8. When partners have read their Book Bits to each other, each should find a different partner and repeat the procedure.
9. Continue this process until students have shared with several partners. You may want to tell students how many partners to share with. For example, "After you have shared your Book Bits with five classmates, return to your seats."
10. Have students return to their desks and write a new prediction based on the new information they have gathered.
11. Repeat steps 7–10.
12. Invite the group or class to share their predictions, how their predictions changed, or any questions they developed during the sharing.
13. Encourage some students to read their Book Bits aloud to support their predictions.
14. Have students read the text from which the Book Bits were taken.

15. After reading, invite students to respond to the selection with questions or connections they made as a result of the reading. You may choose to use the Book Bits reproducible on page 122.

Evaluation

- Quality of responses on the Book Bits reproducible
- Quality of the expressive reading to partners
- Accuracy in reading the Book Bits

Writing Predictions

© R_Tee/Shutterstock.com

Name ________________________________ Date ______________

Title ____

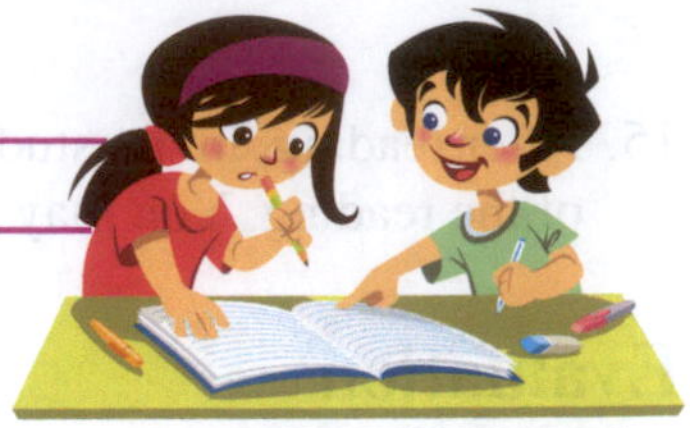
© Thodoris Tibilis/Shutterstock.com

Book Bits

Before Reading

I think this will be about ______________________________

____

____

____

____

Now I think ______________________________________

____

____

____

I predict that ______________________________________

____

____

____

____

After Reading

This is what I think now ______________________________

____

____

____

Here are some questions I still have ______________________

____

____

____

____

Radio Reading

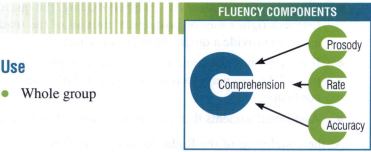

Materials

- Reading selection
- Microphone or toy karaoke machine (recommended for greater engagement)

Use

- Whole group

Description

Radio Reading provides an opportunity for students to use their experiences with audio-only technology to model fluent reading and communicate a message to their peers (Greene, 1979; Searfoss, 1975). In Radio Reading, students read fluently for the purpose of performing and sharing a selected portion of text with others. Just as radio announcers do, they must read with expression at a comprehensible rate so that the listener can focus on the meaning and possible enjoyment of the passage. The procedure has four components: 1) getting started, 2) communicating the message, 3) checking for understanding, and 4) clarifying an unclear message (Searfoss, 1975). Opitz and Rasinski (2008) adapted the original procedure to allow students to practice preselected text prior to reading it aloud. For each portion of the text, one student assumes the role of the radio announcer, and the other students assume the roles of the radio listeners, just as they would when listening to an actual radio broadcast. Only the reader and the teacher have copies of the text open during the reading. All other students are active listeners with books closed. Allowing the reader to hold a microphone or use a toy karaoke machine should enhance the fun and increase motivation.

Procedure

1. Select material that is at the student's instructional level. Materials at the student's instructional level are typically read with 95% accuracy.

2. On the day preceding the Radio Reading experience, explain the procedure to students. Emphasize that it is the reader's responsibility to communicate a message, much like a radio announcer does. Assign segments of text to students to prepare for the next day. These segments might be from a story the group has read, from a trade book or chapter book, from content area material, or from a student periodical.

3. Provide opportunities for students to practice their segments. This practice might be done with a buddy at school or with a parent or sibling at home.

4. In addition to practicing the selection, invite each student to prepare a question or two about the material that can be posed to the listeners following the reading. The questions might be literal or more open-ended, leading to discussion possibilities.

5. On the day you use Radio Reading, review with students the procedures listed below (and summarized on page 125) before beginning the session.

   - The reader reads the assigned passage aloud with meaning and expression.

   - If the reader miscalls a word, the reader is to correct it and go on reading, keeping the flow of the reading, and thus the meaning, intact.

   - If the reader hesitates and can't quickly say a word, the reader may ask the teacher, "What is that word?" The teacher should immediately supply the word, thus preserving the message of the passage for listeners. If the reader hesitates and does not ask for help, the teacher waits a predetermined amount of time for the reader to supply the word (perhaps 5 seconds) and then tells the student the word.

- When the first student has finished reading, the questions he or she has prepared may be asked of the listeners right away or postponed until all of the reading has been completed. Listeners could also be asked to provide a quick summary of what they heard.
- If a reader has not communicated the message of the passage clearly or there is some confusion on the part of the listeners, then the reader is asked to reread the portion of text to help clarify and correct the confusion.
- Additional students then take turns reading their text segments for the listeners.

6. At the conclusion of the Radio Reading experience, each student then poses their questions to the group if they haven't already done so, or you may lead a brief discussion about the entire text. At this time, it may also be appropriate to reflect on the elements of effective read-alouds and how the group did in modeling them during the day's lesson.

Evaluation

- Quality of questions and discussion
- Appropriate emphasis and expression
- Accuracy of word identification
- Quality of rereading to correct confusions

Practicing for Radio Reading

© R_Tee/Shutterstock.com

1. Read your selection aloud with meaning and expression.

2. If you have trouble with a word:
   - correct it and go on.
   - ask, "What is that word?"

3. After reading:
   - ask the questions you have prepared for your selection.
   - ask someone to tell what your selection was mainly about.
   - reread portions of text to clarify and correct confusions.

Appendices

Appendix A

Answers to Anticipation Guide for Fluency

Answers to Anticipation Guide for Fluency

Directions

Compare our notes to your initial impressions on the Anticipation Guide on page 2.

	AFTER READING	
	T or F	**Question(s)**
1. The role of fluency in reading programs has remained the same over the years.	F	1, 10
2. Fluency is independent of comprehension.	F	2
3. Fluency in reading is most relevant at the beginning stages of reading.	F	2, 3
4. It is appropriate to consider fluency in silent reading.	T	4
5. One aspect of fluency can be judged by determining the student's rate of reading in words per minute (WPM).	T	5, 6
6. A reasonable oral fluency rate for third-grade students is 160 words correct per minute (WCPM) by the end of the school year.	T	6
7. Rate of reading is the most important component of fluency.	F	2, 3, 4
8. Fluency should be assessed informally as part of the regular classroom routine.	T	8
9. Round-robin oral reading is an effective fluency activity.	F	9
10. Fluency strategies are primarily for students experiencing difficulty in reading.	F	10, 12
11. Research has identified several methods to increase reading fluency.	T	11, 12
12. Oral reading fluency is developed best through independent reading.	F	14
13. Fluency instruction should begin after students have established conventional reading, typically in second grade.	F	13
14. Some teacher behaviors can contribute to students' dysfluency in reading.	T	14
15. Fluency strategies and interventions can be differentiated.	T	14, 15

From Melanie Walski, Peet Smith, Jerry L. Johns, and Roberta L. Berglund, *Fluency: Questions, Answers, and Evidence-Based Strategies* (5th ed.). Copyright © 2020 Kendall Hunt Publishing Company. May be reproduced for noncommercial educational purposes.

Appendix B

Resources for Assessing and Monitoring Fluency Progress

Appendix B provides you with a variety of resources to help you informally assess students' fluency and ways to record and monitor progress and growth in areas of fluency.

Four-Point Fluency Rubric

	1	2	3	4
Comprehension	Questions—less than 60% Retelling—few major ideas, poor accuracy, poor ordering.	Questions—60%–74% Retelling includes some ideas, not fully accurate or well-ordered.	Questions—75%–89% Retelling is mostly complete, accurate, and well-ordered.	Questions—90% or more Retelling is fully complete, accurate, and well-ordered.
Accuracy	90% or less	91% to 94%	95% to 98%	99% to 100%
Rate	Slow and laborious; struggles with words.	Rate varies; some hesitations.	Generally conversational; rate varies as appropriate.	Reads at conversational pace throughout.
Prosody	Reads with monotone; does not sound like natural speech; little or no use of punctuation.	Mostly monotone; sometimes voice matches interpretation of the passage; some use of punctuation.	Reads with expression and uses punctuation most of the time; voice matches interpretation of the passage.	Reads with varied volume and expression; voice matches interpretation of the passage and punctuation is used consistently.

From Melanie Walski, Peet Smith, Jerry L. Johns, and Roberta L. Berglund, *Fluency: Questions, Answers, and Evidence-Based Strategies* (5th ed.). Copyright © 2020 Kendall Hunt Publishing Company. May be reproduced for noncommercial educational purposes.

Student _____ Selection _____ Level _____ Date _____

Four-Point Fluency Rubric for Oral Reading

FOCUS	1	2	3	4
Rate	Slow and laborious Struggles with words	Rate varies Some hesitations	Generally conversational Some smooth, some choppy	Conversational and consistent Smooth and fluent throughout
Prosody	Monotone	Monotone combined with some expression	Appropriate expression used much of the time	Appropriate expression maintained throughout
Phrasing	Word-by-word Long pauses between words	Some word-by-word, some phrases	Mostly phrases, some smooth, some choppy	Phrases consistently throughout generally smooth and fluent
Punctuation	Little or no use	Uses some Ignores some	Uses most of the time	Uses consistently throughout

Suggestions for Rubric Use:

You may wish to choose one area for assessing a student's progress (for example, rate, prosody, phrasing, or punctuation), or you may wish to score a student's reading in all four areas. If you wish to score a student's multiple readings of a selection, you may wish to highlight each reading with a different color. For example, after the first reading, circle the words for the score for each area you are checking in yellow. The next time you check the student on the same passage, use a blue highlighter, and the third time a green highlighter to check (✔) your ratings. You and the student can easily see if progress is being made in one or several areas as a result of the multiple rereadings.

Record your color-coding below.

First reading _____

Second reading _____

Third reading _____

From Melanie Walski, Peet Smith, Jerry L. Johns, and Roberta L. Berglund, *Fluency: Questions, Answers, and Evidence-Based Strategies* (5th ed.). Copyright © 2020 Kendall Hunt Publishing Company. May be reproduced for noncommercial educational purposes.

Holistic Oral Reading Fluency Scale

Fluent	Level 4	Reads primarily in larger, meaningful phrase groups. Although some regressions, repetitions, and deviations from text may be present, these do not appear to detract from the overall structure of the story. Preservation of the author's syntax is consistent. Some or most of the story is read with expressive interpretation.
	Level 3	Reads primarily in three- or four-word phrase groups. Some small groupings may be present. However, the majority of the phrasing seems appropriate and preserves the syntax of the author. Little or no expressive interpretation is present.
Nonfluent	Level 2	Reads primarily in two-word phrases with some three- or four-word groupings. Some word-by-word reading may be present. Word groupings may seem awkward and unrelated to larger context of sentence or passage.
	Level 1	Reads primarily word-by-word. Occasional two-word or three-word phrases may occur—but these are infrequent and/or they do not preserve meaningful syntax.

U.S. Department of Education, Institute of Education Sciences, National Center for Education Statistics. National Assessment for Educational Progress (NAEP), 2002, Oral Reading Study.

From Melanie Walski, Peet Smith, Jerry L. Johns, and Roberta L. Berglund, *Fluency: Questions, Answers, and Evidence-Based Strategies* (5th ed.). Copyright © 2020 Kendall Hunt Publishing Company. May be reproduced for noncommercial educational purposes.

Class Fluency Snapshot—Primary Grades

Teacher _____ Grade _____ Circle Text Type Narrative
Informational

Date _____	Date _____	Date _____
Passage _____	Passage _____	Passage _____
Level _____	Level _____	Level _____

180
170
160
150
140
130
120
110
100
90
80
70
60
50
40
30
≤20

180
170
160
150
140
130
120
110
100
90
80
70
60
50
40
30
≤20

180
170
160
150
140
130
120
110
100
90
80
70
60
50
40
30
≤20

WCPM   WCPM   WCPM

Class Fluency Snapshot—Upper Grades

Teacher _____ Grade _____ Circle Text Type Narrative Informational

Date _____	Date _____	Date _____
Passage _____	Passage _____	Passage _____
Level _____	Level _____	Level _____

220 210 200 190 180 170 160 150 140 130 120 110 100 90 80 70 60 ≤50

220 210 200 190 180 170 160 150 140 130 120 110 100 90 80 70 60 ≤50

220 210 200 190 180 170 160 150 140 130 120 110 100 90 80 70 60 ≤50

WCPM   WCPM   WCPM

Cumulative Record for Fluency Checks

GRADE	DATE _____ FIRST READING			DATE _____ SECOND READING			DATE _____ THIRD READING		
	WCPM	COMP.	EXP.	WCPM	COMP.	EXP.	WCPM	COMP.	EXP.
1 _____ Teacher									
2 _____ Teacher									
3 _____ Teacher									
4 _____ Teacher									
5 _____ Teacher									
6 _____ Teacher									
7 _____ Teacher									
8 _____ Teacher									

WCPM = Words Correct Per Minute

Comp. = Comprehension (Good, Fair, Poor based on your judgment)

Exp. = Expression (Good, Fair, Poor or use rubric on page 133)

Class Record of Fluency Progress Monitoring

Teacher _____

Title _____

Grade Level: 1 2 3 4 5 6 (Circle One)

Text Type: Narrative Informational (Circle One)

Reading Level _____

STUDENT	RATE (WCPM)			ACCURACY % CORRECT			COMPREHENSION % CORRECT			PROSODY (1–4)		
	FALL	WINTER	SPRING	FALL	WINTER	SPRING	FALL	WINTER	SPRING	FALL	WINTER	SPRING

References

Adams, M. J. (1990). *Beginning to read: Thinking and learning about print*. Cambridge, MA: MIT Press.

Allington, R. L. (2001). *What really matters for struggling readers: Designing research-based programs*. New York: Longman.

Allington, R. L. (2006). Fluency: Still waiting after all these years. In S. J. Samuels & A. E. Farstrup (Eds.), *What research has to say about fluency instruction* (pp. 94–105). Newark, DE: International Reading Association.

Allington, R. L. (2009). *What really matters in fluency*. New York: Pearson.

Allington, R. L. (2014). How reading volume affects both reading fluency and reading achievement. *International Electronic Journal of Elementary Education, 7,* 13–26.

Anderson, C. A. (2000). Sustained silent reading: Try it, you'll like it. *The Reading Teacher, 54,* 258–259.

Anderson, R. C., Hiebert, E. H., Scott, J. A., & Wilkinson, I. A. G. (1985). *Becoming a nation of readers: The report of the Commission on Reading*. Washington, DC: The National Institute of Education.

Applegate, M. D., Applegate, A. J., & Modla, V. B. (2009). "She's my best reader; she just can't comprehend": Studying the relationship between fluency and comprehension. *The Reading Teacher, 62,* 512–521.

Armbruster, B. B., Lehr, F., & Osborn, J. (2001). *Put reading first: The research building blocks for teaching children to read*. Jessup, MD: National Institute for Literacy.

Ash, G. E., & Kuhn, M. R. (2006). Meaningful oral and silent reading in the elementary and middle school classroom. In T. Rasinski, C. Blachowicz, & K. Lems (Eds.), *Fluency instruction: Research-based best practices* (pp. 155–172). New York: Guilford.

Baker, S. K., Beattie, T., Nelson, N. J., & Turtura, J. (2018). *How we learn to read: The critical role of phonological awareness*. Washington, DC: U.S. Department of Education, Office of Elementary and Secondary Education, Office of Special Education Programs, National Center on Improving Literacy. Retrieved from http://improvingliteracy.org

Bear, D. R., & Barone, D. (1998). *Developing literacy: An integrated approach to assessment and instruction*. Boston: Houghton Mifflin.

Berglund, R. L. (1988). Shared book experience: Bridging the gap between lap reading and school reading. *Wisconsin State Reading Association Journal, 31,* 23–32.

Berglund, R. L., & Johns, J. L. (1983). A primer on uninterrupted sustained silent reading. *The Reading Teacher, 36,* 534–539.

Blachman, B. A. (2000). Phonological awareness. In M. L. Kamil, P. B. Mosenthal, P. D. Pearson, & R. Barr (Eds.), *Handbook of reading research* (Vol. III) (pp. 483–502). Mahwah, NJ: Erlbaum.

Blachowicz, C. L. Z., Sullivan, D. M., & Cieply, C. (2001). Fluency snapshots: A quick screening tool for your classroom. *Reading Psychology, 22,* 95–109.

Block, C., & Mangieri, J. (2002). Recreational reading: 20 years later. *The Reading Teacher, 55,* 572–580.

Breznitz, Z. (2006). *Fluency in reading: Synchronization of processes*. Mahwah, NJ: Erlbaum.

Burns, B. (2001). *Guided reading: A how-to for all grades*. Arlington Heights, IL: SkyLight.

Burns, M. S., Griffin, P., & Snow, C. E. (Eds.) (1999). *Starting out right: A guide to promoting children's reading success*. Washington, DC: National Academy Press.

Carver, R. P. (1989). Silent reading rates in grade equivalents. *Journal of Reading Behavior, 21,* 155–166.

Chung, M., & Keckler, B. (2016). Shared-book experience using science-themed books to develop scientific literacy: An interactive approach with struggling readers. *Language and Literacy Spectrum, 26,* 31–40.

Corso, L., Funk, S., & Gaffney, J. (2001/2002). An educational evening out. *The Reading Teacher, 55,* 326–329.

Cowie, R., Douglas-Cowie, E., & Wichmann, A. (2002). Prosodic characteristics of skilled reading: Fluency and expressiveness in 8–10-year-old readers. *Language and Speech, 45,* 47–82.

Cunningham, P. M. (1999). *The teacher's guide to the four blocks.* Greensboro, NC: Carson-Dellosa.

Cunningham, A. E., & Stanovich, K. E. (1998). The impact of print exposure on word recognition. In J. L. Metsala & L. C. Ehri (Eds.), *Word recognition in beginning literacy* (pp. 235–262). Mahwah, NJ: Lawrence Erlbaum Associates.

Cunningham, P. M. & Hall, D. P. (2009). *Making words 1st grade: 100 hands-on lessons for phonemic awareness, phonics, and spelling.* Upper Saddle River, NJ: Pearson.

Cunningham, P. M. & Hall, D. P. (2009). *Making words 2nd grade: 100 hands-on lessons for phonemic awareness, phonics, and spelling.* Upper Saddle River, NJ: Pearson.

Cunningham, P. M. & Hall, D. P. (2009). *Making words 3rd grade: 100 hands-on lessons for phonemic awareness, phonics, and spelling.* Upper Saddle River, NJ: Pearson.

Cunningham, P. M. & Hall, D. P. (2009). *Making words 4th grade: 100 hands-on lessons for phonemic awareness, phonics, and spelling.* Upper Saddle River, NJ: Pearson.

Daane, M. C., Campbell, J. R., Grigg, W. S., Goodman, M. J., & Oranje, A. (2005). Fourth-grade students reading aloud: NAEP 2002 Special Study of Oral Reading (NCES 2006-469). U.S. Department of Education. Institute of Education Sciences, National Center for Education Statistics. Washington, DC: Government Printing Office.

deRegniers, B. S. (1988). *Sing a song of popcorn: Every child's book of poems.* New York: Scholastic.

Ehri, L., Nunes, S. R., Willows, D. M., Schuster, B. V., Yaghoub-Zadeh, Z., & Shanahan, T. (2001). Phonemic awareness instruction helps children learn to read: Evidence from the National Reading Panel's meta-analysis. *Reading Research Quarterly 36,* 250–287.

Eldredge, J. L., Reutzel, D. R., & Hollingsworth, P. M. (1996). Comparing the effectiveness of two oral reading practices: Round-robin reading and the shared book experience. *Journal of Literacy Research, 28,* 201–225.

Elley, W. B. (1988). Vocabulary acquisition from listening to stories. *Reading Research Quarterly, 24,* 174–187.

Faver, S. (2008/2009). Repeated reading of poetry can enhance reading fluency. *The Reading Teacher, 62,* 350–352.

Flood, J., Lapp, D., & Fisher, D. (2005). Neurological impress methods plus. *Reading Psychology, 26,* 147–150.

Flynn, R. M. (2004/2005). Curriculum-based readers theatre: Setting the stage for reading and retention. *The Reading Teacher, 58,* 360–365.

Fountas, I. C., & Pinnell, G. S. (2000). *Matching books to readers: Using leveled books in guided reading, K–3.* Portsmouth, NH: Heinemann.

Fountas, I. C., & Pinnell, G. S. (2001). *Guiding readers and writers: Grades 3–6.* Portsmouth, NH: Heinemann.

Fox, B. J. (2007). *Word identification strategies: Building phonics into a classroom reading program* (4th ed.). New York: Prentice Hall.

Fox, B. J. (2014). *Phonics and words study for the teacher of reading* (11th ed.). Upper Saddle River, NJ: Pearson.

Gardiner, S. (2005). *Building student literacy through sustained silent reading.* Alexandria, VA: Association for Supervision and Curriculum Development.

Genishi, C., & Dyson, A. H. (2009). *Children, language, and literacy: Diverse learners in diverse times.* New York: Teacher's College Press.

Gillet, J. W., Temple, C., & Crawford, A. N. (2004). *Understanding reading problems: Assessment and instruction* (6th ed.). Boston: Allyn and Bacon.

Gillet, J. W., Temple, C. A., Temple, C., & Crawford, A. (2016). *Understanding reading problems: Assessment and instruction* (9th ed.). Upper Saddle River, NJ: Pearson.

Greene, F. (1979). Radio reading. In C. Pennock (Ed.), *Reading comprehension at four linguistic levels* (pp. 104–107). Newark, DE: International Reading Association.

Gunning, T. G. (2000). *Best books for building literacy for elementary school children.* Boston: Allyn and Bacon.

Gunning, T. G. (2011). *Reading success for all students: Using formative assessment to guide instruction and intervention.* Indianapolis, IN: Jossey-Bass.

Guthrie, J. T. (2004). Teaching for literacy engagement. *Journal of Literacy Research, 36,* 1–28.

Guthrie, J. T., & Cox, K. E. (2001). Classroom conditions for motivation and engagement. *Educational Psychology Review, 13,* 283–302.

Guthrie, J. T., Hoa, L. W., Wigfield, A., Tonks, S. M., & Perencevich, K. C. (2006). From spark to fire: Can situational reading interest lead to long-term reading motivation? *Reading Research and Instruction, 45,* 91–117.

Hall, D. P., & Cunningham, P. M. (2009). *Making words grade K: 100 hands-on lessons for phonemic awareness, phonics, and spelling.* Upper Saddle River, NJ: Pearson.

Harris, T. L., & Hodges, R. E. (Eds.) (1995). *The literacy dictionary: The vocabulary of reading and writing.* Newark, DE: International Reading Association.

Hasbrouck, J., & Tindal, G. A. (2006). Oral reading fluency norms: A valuable assessment tool for reading teachers. *The Reading Teacher, 59,* 636–644.

Hasbrouck, J., & Tindal, G. A. (2017). *An update to compiled ORF norms.* Eugene, OR: Behavioral Research and Teaching, University of Oregon.

Heckelman, R. G. (1969). A neurological-impress method of remedial-reading instruction. *Academic Therapy Quarterly, 4,* 277–282.

Heilman, A. W., Blair, T. R., & Rupley, W. H. (2002). *Principles and practices of teaching reading* (10th ed.). Upper Saddle River, NJ: Merrill Prentice-Hall.

Herrell, A. L. (2000). *Fifty strategies for teaching English language learners.* Upper Saddle River, NJ: Prentice-Hall.

Hiebert, E. H., Samuels, S. J., & Rasinski, T. V. (2012). Comprehension-based silent reading rates: What do we know? What do we need to know? *Literacy Research and Instruction, 51,* 110–124.

Hyatt, A. V. (1943). *The place of oral reading in the school program: Its history and development from 1880–1941.* New York: Teachers College Press.

Indiana Library Federation. (2001). *Read-aloud books too good to miss.* http://www.ilfonline.org/Programs/ReadAloud/readaloud.htm

International Literacy Association. (2018). *Exploring the 2017 NAEP reading results: Systemic reforms beat simplistic solutions* [Literacy leadership brief]. Newark, DE: Author.

International Literacy Association. (2018). *Reading fluently does not mean reading fast* [Literacy leadership brief]. Newark, DE: Author.

International Literacy Association. (2018). *What's hot in literacy report.* Newark, DE: Author.

Johns, J. L. (1975). Dolch list of common nouns—A comparison. *The Reading Teacher, 28,* 338–340.

Johns, J. L. (1976). Updating the Dolch basic sight vocabulary. *Reading Horizons, 16,* 104–111.

Johns, J. L., Elish-Piper, L., & Johns, B. (2017). *Basic reading inventory* (12th ed.). Dubuque, IA: Kendall Hunt.

Johns, J. L., & Lenski, S. D. (2010). *Improving reading: Interventions, strategies, and resources* (5th ed.). Dubuque, IA: Kendall Hunt.

Johns, J. L., & Lenski, S. D. (2019). *Improving reading: Strategies, resources, and common core connections* (7th ed.). Dubuque, IA: Kendall Hunt.

Johnson, L., Graham, S., & Harris, K. R. (1997). The effects of goal setting and self-instruction on learning a reading comprehension strategy: A study of students with learning disabilities. *Journal of Learning Disabilities, 30,* 80–90.

Keehn, S. (2003). The effect of instruction and practice through readers theatre on young readers' oral reading fluency. *Reading Research and Instruction, 42,* 40–61.

Keene, E. O. (2008). *To understand: New horizons in reading comprehension.* Portsmouth, NH: Heinemann.

Keene, E. O., & Zimmermann, S. (1997). *Mosaic of thought.* Portsmouth, NH: Heinemann.

Klenk, L., & Kibby, M. L. (2000). Re-mediating reading difficulties: Appraising the past, reconciling the present, constructing the future. In M. L. Kamil, P. B. Mosenthal, P. D. Pearson, & R. Barr (Eds.), *Handbook of reading research* (Vol. III) (pp. 667–690). Mahwah, NJ: Erlbaum.

Krashen, S. D. (2004). *The power of reading: Insights from the research* (2nd ed.). Portsmouth, NH: Heinemann.

Kuhn, M. (2004/2005). Helping students become accurate, expressive readers: Fluency instruction for small groups. *The Reading Teacher, 58,* 338–344.

Kuhn, M. R., & Stahl, S. A. (2000). *Fluency: A review of developmental and remedial practices.* Ann Arbor, MI: Center for the Improvement of Early Reading Achievement.

Kuhn, M. R., Schwanenflugel, P. J., Meisinger, E. B., Levy, B. A., & Rasinski, T. V. (2010). Aligning theory and assessment of reading fluency: Automaticity, prosody, and definitions of fluency. *Reading Research Quarterly, 45,* 230-251.

LaBerge, D., & Samuels, S. J. (1974). Toward a theory of automatic information processing in reading. *Cognitive Psychology, 6,* 293–323.

Layne, S. L. (1996). *Vocabulary acquisition by fourth-grade students from listening to teachers' oral reading of novels.* Unpublished doctoral dissertation, Northern Illinois University, DeKalb.

Mahar M. T., Murphy, S. K., Rowe, D. A., Golden, J., Shields, A. T., & Raedeke, T. D. (2006). Effects of a classroom-based program on physical activity and on-task behavior. *Medicine and Science in Sports and Exercise, 38,* 2086–2094.

Mallon, B., & Berglund, R. L. (1984). The language experience approach to reading: Recurring questions and their answers. *The Reading Teacher, 37,* 867–871.

Maro, N. (2001). Reading to improve fluency. *Illinois Reading Council Journal, 29*(3), 10–18.

Maro, N. (2004). *Personal communication,* August 13, 2004.

Martin, B., Jr. (1987). *Brown bear, brown bear, what do you see?* New York: Holt.

Martinez, M., Roser, N. L., & Strecker, S. (1998/1999). "I never thought I could be a star:" A readers theatre ticket to fluency. *The Reading Teacher, 52,* 326–334.

McCormick, S. (2007). *Instructing students who have literacy problems* (5th ed.). Upper Saddle River, NJ: Merrill Prentice Hall.

Miller, J., & Schwanenflugel, P. J. (2006). Prosody of syntactically complex sentences in the oral reading of young children. *Journal of Educational Psychology, 98,* 839–853.

Miller, J., & Schwanenflugel, P. J. (2008). A longitudinal study of the development of reading prosody as a dimension of oral reading fluency in early elementary school children. *Reading Research Quarterly, 43,* 336–354.

Monobe, G., Bintz, W. P., & McTeer, J. S. (2017). Developing English learners' reading confidence with whole class repeated reading. *The Reading Teacher, 71,* 347–350.

Moskal, M. K. (2005/2006). Student self-selected repeated reading: Successful fluency development for disfluent readers. *Illinois Reading Council Journal, 34*(1), 3–11.

Moskal, M. K., & Blachowicz, C. (2006). *Partnering for fluency.* New York: Guilford.

National Governors Association. (2010). Common Core State Standards. Washington DC: National Governors Association Center for Best Practices, Council of Chief State School Officers.

National Reading Panel (2000). *Teaching children to read: An evidenced-based assessment of the scientific research literature on reading and its implications for reading instruction.* Washington, DC: National Institute of Child Health and Human Development.

NELP (National Early Literacy Panel). 2008. *Developing Early Literacy: Report of the National Early Literacy Panel.* Washington, DC: National Institute for Literacy.

Ness, M. (2009). Laughing through rereadings: Using joke books to build fluency. *The Reading Teacher, 62,* 691–694.

O'Connor, R. E., Bell, K. M., Harty, K. R., Larkin, L. K., Sacker, S. M., & Zigmond, N. (2002). Teaching reading to poor readers in the intermediate grades: A comparison of text difficulty. *Journal of Educational Psychology, 94,* 474–485.

Opitz, M. F., & Ford, M. P. (2001). *Reaching readers: Flexible & innovative strategies for guided reading.* Portsmouth, NH: Heinemann.

Opitz, M. F., & Rasinski, T. (1998). *Good-bye round robin: 25 effective oral reading strategies.* Portsmouth, NH: Heinemann.

Opitz, M. F., & Rasinski, T. (2008). *Good-bye round robin, updated edition.* Portsmouth, NH: Heinemann.

Padak, N. D., & Rasinski, T. V. (2008). *Evidence-based instruction in reading: A professional development guide to fluency.* New York: Pearson.

Pearson, P. D., & Fielding, L. (1991). Comprehension instruction. In R. Barr, M. L. Kamil, P. Mosenthal, & P. D. Pearson (Eds.), *Handbook of reading research* (Vol. II) (pp. 815–860). New York: Longman.

Person, M. E. (1993). Say it right! In M. W. Olson & S. P. Homan (Eds.), *Teacher to teacher: Strategies for the elementary classroom* (pp. 37–38). Newark, DE: International Reading Association.

Pilgreen, J. (2000). *The SSR handbook: How to organize and manage a Sustained Silent Reading program.* Portsmouth, NH: Heinemann.

Pinnell, G. S., & Fountas, I. C. (2002). *Leveled books for readers, grades 3–6.* Portsmouth, NH: Heinemann.

Pinnell, G. S., Pikulski, J. J., Wixson, K. K., Campbell, J. R., Gough, P. B., & Beatty, A. S. (1995). *Listening to children read aloud.* Washington, DC: Office of Educational Research and Improvement, U.S. Department of Education.

Rasinski, T. (2006). Reading fluency instruction: Moving beyond accuracy, automaticity, and prosody. *The Reading Teacher, 59,* 704–706.

Rasinski, T., Rikli, A., & Johnston, S. (2009). Reading fluency: More than automaticity? More than a concern for the primary grades? *Literacy Research and Instruction, 48,* 350–361.

Rasinski, T., Yildirim, K., & Nageldinger, J. (2011). Building fluency through the phrased text lesson. *The Reading Teacher, 65,* 252–255.

Rasinski, T. V. (1990). Effects of repeated reading and listening-while-reading on reading fluency. *The Journal of Educational Research, 83,* 147–150.

Rasinski, T. V. (2000). Speed does matter in reading. *The Reading Teacher, 54,* 146–151.

Rasinski, T. V. (2017). Readers who struggle: Why many struggle and a modest proposal for improving their reading. *The Reading Teacher, 70,* 519–524.

Rasinski, T. V., & Hoffman, J. V. (2003). Oral reading in the school curriculum. *Reading Research Quarterly, 38,* 510–522.

Rasinski, T. V. & Padak, N. D. (1996). *Holistic reading strategies: Teaching students who find reading difficult.* Englewood Cliffs, NJ: Merrill.

Rasinski, T. V., Padak, N. D., Linek, W. L., & Sturtevant, B. (1994). Effects of fluency development on urban second-grade readers. *The Journal of Educational Research, 87,* 158–165.

Rasinski, T. V., Padak, N. D., McKeon, C. A., Wilfong, L. G., Friedauer, J. A., & Heim, P. (2005). Is reading fluency a key for successful high school reading? *Journal of Adolescent & Adult Reading, 40,* 22–27.

Reutzel, D. R., & Hollingsworth, P. M. (1993). Effects of fluency training on second graders' reading comprehension. *Journal of Educational Research, 86,* 325–331.

Reutzel, D. R., Hollingsworth, P. M., & Eldredge, L. (1994). Oral reading instruction: The impact on student reading comprehension. *Journal of Educational Research, 86,* 325–331.

Reutzel, D. R., & Juth, S. (2014). Supporting the development of silent reading fluency: An evidence-based framework for the intermediate grades (3–6). *International Electronic Journal of Elementary Education, 7,* 27–46.

Roser, N. L. (2001). *Supporting the literacy of bilingual middle graders with culturally relevant readers theatre scripts.* Paper presented at the 46th Annual Convention of the International Reading Association, New Orleans, LA.

Routman, R. (2000). *Conversations: Strategies for teaching, learning, and evaluating.* Portsmouth, NH: Heinemann.

RTI: Questions reading professionals should ask. (2009, August/September). *Reading Today, 27* (1), 1, 6.

Samuels, S. J. (1979). The method of repeated readings. *The Reading Teacher, 32,* 403–408.

Samuels, S. J. (2002). Reading fluency: Its development and assessment. In A. E. Farstrup & S. J. Samuels (Eds.), *What research has to say about reading instruction* (3rd ed.) (pp. 166–183). Newark, DE: International Reading Association.

Samuels, S. J. (2006). Toward a model of reading fluency. In S. J. Samuels & A. E. Farstrup (Eds.), *What research has to say about fluency instruction* (pp. 24–46). Newark, DE: International Reading Association.

Santoro, L. E., Chard, D. J., Howard, L., & Baker, S. K. (2008). Making the very most of classroom readalouds to promote comprehension and vocabulary. *The Reading Teacher, 61*, 396–408.

Scheffel, T. L., & Booth, D. (2013). Towards literacy growth and community participation: Lessons learned from a shared book experience in one Northern Ontario community. *Literacy Learning: The Middle Years, 21*, 35–40.

Schwanenflugel, P. J., Hamilton, A. M., Kuhn, M. R., Wisenbaker, J. M., & Stahl, S. A. (2004). Becoming a fluent reader: Reading skill and prosodic features in the oral reading of young readers. *Journal of Educational Psychology, 96*, 119–129.

Schwanenflugel, P. J., Westmoreland, M. R., & Benjamin, R. (2015). Reading fluency skill and the prosodic marking of linguistic focus. *Reading and Writing: An Interdisciplinary Journal, 28*, 9–30.

Searfoss, L. (1975). Radio reading. *The Reading Teacher, 29*, 295–296.

Shanahan, T. (2000). *Literacy teaching framework.* Unpublished manuscript, University of Illinois at Chicago.

Shepard, A. (1997). *From stories to stage: Tips for reader's theatre.* http://www.aaronshep.com/rt/Tips3.

Short, D., & Echevarria, J. (2004). Teacher skills to support English Language Learners. *Educational Leadership, 62*, 9–13.

Sindelar, P. T., Monda, L. E., & O'Shea, L. J. (1990). Effects of repeated readings on instructional- and mastery-level readers. *Journal of Educational Research, 83*, 220–226.

Stanley, N. (2004). A celebration of words. *Teaching Pre-K–8, 34*(7), 56–57.

Stanovich, K. E. (1993). The language code: Issues in word recognition. In S. R. Yussen & M. C. Smith (Eds.), *Reading across the life span* (pp. 111–135). Hillsdale, NJ: Erlbaum.

Strickland, D. S., Ganske, K., & Monroe, J. K. (2002). *Supporting struggling readers and writers: Strategies for classroom interventions 3–6.* Newark, DE: International Reading Association.

Sullivan, J. (2004). *The children's literature lover's book of lists.* San Francisco: Jossey-Bass.

Teale, W. H., & Shanahan, T. (2001). Ignoring the essential: Myths about fluency. *Illinois Reading Council Journal, 29*(3), 5–8.

Topping, K. (1987a). Paired reading: A powerful technique for parent use. *The Reading Teacher, 40*, 608–614.

Topping, K. (1987b). Peer tutored paired reading: Outcome data from ten projects. *Educational Psychology, 7*, 604–614.

Topping, K. (1989). Peer tutoring and paired reading: Combining two powerful techniques. *The Reading Teacher, 42*, 488–494.

Topping, K. J. (2006). Building reading fluency: Cognitive, behavioral, and socioemotional factors and the role of peer-mediated learning. In S. J. Samuels & A. E. Farstrup (Eds.), *What research has to say about fluency instruction* (pp. 106–129). Newark, DE: International Reading Association.

Torgesen, J. K. (2004). Lessons learned from research on interventions for students who have difficulty learning to read. In P. McCardle & V. Chhabra (Eds.), *The voice of evidence in reading research* (pp. 355–382). Baltimore: Paul H. Brooks.

Torgesen, J. K., & Hudson, R. F. (2006). Reading fluency: Critical issues for readers who struggle. In S. J. Samuels & A. E. Farstrup (Eds.), *What research has to say about fluency instruction* (pp. 130–158). Newark, DE: International Reading Association.

Vazou, S., Gavrilou, P., Mamalaki, E., Papanastasiou, A., & Sioumala, N. (2012). Does integrating physical activity in the elementary school classroom influence academic motivation? *International Journal of Sport and Exercise Psychology, 10,* 251–263.

Whitehurst, G. J., & Lonigan, C. J. (1998). Child development and emergent literacy. *Child Development, 69,* 848–872.

Worthy, J., & Broaddus, K. (2001/2002). Fluency beyond the primary grades: From group performance to silent, independent reading. *The Reading Teacher, 55,* 334–343.

Yopp, H. K., & Yopp, R. H. (2000). Supporting phonemic awareness development in the classroom. *The Reading Teacher, 54,* 130–143.

Yopp, R. H., & Yopp, H. K. (2003). Time with text. *The Reading Teacher, 57,* 284–287.

Young, T. A., & Vardell, S. (1993). Weaving readers theatre and nonfiction into the curriculum. *The Reading Teacher, 46,* 396–406.

Ziadat, A. H., & AL-Awan, M. S. (2018). The effectiveness of neurological impress method on reading fluency of students with learning disabilities in Amman, Jordan. *International Education Studies, 11,* 165–171.

Index

READING TITLES BY AWARD-WINNING AUTHORS

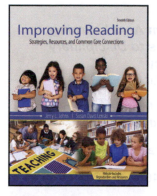

Improving Reading: Strategies, Resources, and Common Core Connections
7th Edition

Jerry Johns & Susan Lenski

he.kendallhunt.com/ir

978-1-5249-5957-9

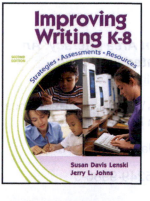

Improving Writing K-8: Strategies, Assessments, Resources
2nd Edition

Susan Lenski & Jerry Johns

he.kendallhunt.com/iw

978-0-7575-0788-5

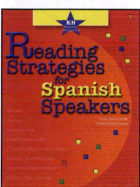

Reading Strategies for Spanish Speakers
1st Edition

Susan Lenski & Fabiola Ehlers-Zavala

he.kendallhunt.com/lenskispanish

978-0-7575-0787-8

Spanish Reading Inventory
2nd Edition

Jerry Johns & Mayra C. Daniel

he.kendallhunt.com/sri

978-0-7575-7591-4

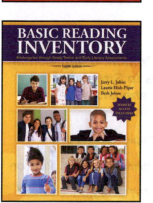

Basic Reading Inventory: Kindergarten through Grade Twelve and Early Literacy Assessments
12th Edition

Jerry Johns, Laurie Eilsh-Piper, & Beth Johns

he.kendallhunt.com/bri

978-1-5249-0562-0

Comprehension and Vocabulary Strategies for the Elementary Grades w/ CD ROM
2nd Edition

Jerry Johns, Susan Lenski & Roberta L. Berglund

he.kendallhunt.com/ece

978-0-7575-2798-2

To request a review copy, complete the form below and return to **Deborah A. Roth, Publishing Solutions Representative, at Kendall Hunt Publishing Company 4050 Westmark Drive, Dubuque, Iowa 52002.**

First Name: _____ Last Name: _____

E-mail address: _____

Street Address: _____ City: _____

State: _____ Zip: _____ ISBN # _____

READING TITLES BY AWARD-WINNING AUTHORS

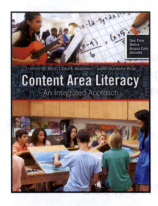

Content Area Literacy: An Integrated Approach
11th Edition

Thomas W. Bean, John Readence, & Judith Dunkerly Bean

he.kendallhunt.com/bean

978-1-5249-9986-5

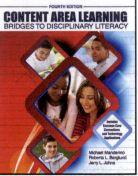

Content Area Learning: Bridges to Disciplinary Literacy
4th Edition

Michael Manderino, Roberta L. Berglund & Jerry Johns

he.kendallhunt.com/manderino

978-1-4652-4162-7

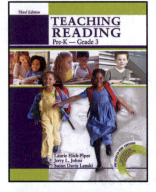

Teaching Reading Pre-K to Grade 3 w/ CD-ROM
3rd Edition

Laurie Elish-Piper, Jerry Johns & Susan Lenski

he.kendallhunt.com/elish_piper

978-0-7575-3876-6

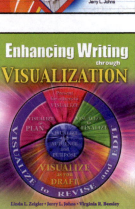

Enhancing Writing Through Visualization
1st Edition

Linda Zeigler, Jerry Johns & Virginia R. Beesley

he.kendallhunt.com/zeigler

978-0-7575-4090-5

Essential Comprehension Strategies for the Intermediate Grade
1st Edition

Jerry Johns, Susan Lenski, & Roberta L. Berglund

he.kendallhunt.com/eci

978-0-7575-8660-6

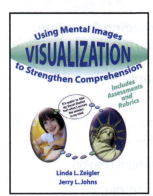

Visualization: Using Mental Images to Strengthen Comprehension
1st Edition

Linda Zeigler & Jerry Johns

he.kendallhunt.com/visualization

978-0-7575-0935-3

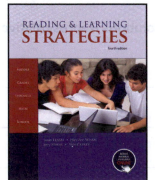

Reading and Learning Strategies: Middle Grades Through High School
4th Edition

Susan Lenski, Mary Ann Wham, Jerry Johns, & Micki M. Caskey

he.kendallhunt.com/lenski_hs

978-0-7575-8812-9

To request a review copy, complete the form and return to **Deborah A. Roth, Publishing Solutions Representative, at Kendall Hunt Publishing Company 4050 Westmark Drive, Dubuque, Iowa 52002.**

Deborah A. Roth
Publishing Solutions Representative
Kendall Hunt Publishing Company
563-589-1087 | Droth@kendallhunt.com

Editions and covers are subject to change. Always check the Kendall Hunt website (http://he.kendallhunt.com) before ordering.